Letters From Children

Awesome, fabulous, fantastic, wonderful, the best! My siblings have become my "bestest" friends. — Lydia, age 14

My sisters and I like (realllllly like) your book. — Hannah, age 10

I want to tell you how much your book has changed me. My mom reads a small part of it every day and I always wish she would keep reading. I believe your book is making me and my brothers and sisters best friends. — Joshua, age 11

Your book has really made our relationships better. — Gwen, age 8

I really liked Stephen's funny stories. I will stop bugging my brothers. — Jason, age 7

I loved your book. But personally I think my brother needs it. — Anonymous

Letters From Organizations and Schools

As a Biblical Christian counselor for over thirty years, I have counseled hundreds of young people .... This book is a tool every family needs. It will help you achieve your goals of family harmony. — Dr. Jim Logan, Intl. Center for Biblical Counseling

It speaks to a critical need for families. We recommend it for families in Illinois. — Illinois Christian Home Educators

A book written by experts, it is a triumph of creative zeal. — Abide Magazine

Easy to read, reflective and full of constructive ideas. — Marion Independent School District

This is a fun-to-read, realistic book and would be an asset to any family's library. — The King's Daughter Magazine

I am using your book for my class in school. When we got to the part on "bitterness," we had a time of prayer where I encouraged each student to ask if there were any people they were bitter against ... One student had tears when he looked up. — Sharon, Teacher

This is a major piece of work. It addresses many biblical and Christlike qualities of life and illustrates them well.
— Dr. Daniel Smith, Chancellor of Emmaus Bible College

Entertaining and effective, a very helpful tool.
— Ray King, Editor of Christian Healthcare Newsletter

LETTERS FROM PARENTS

Our book is so worn and torn and dog-eared. We are missing most of the pages. It is full of encouraging and funny and amazing testimonies.
— Family In Texas

A tremendous blessing to us, it is something that our family really needed. Good stuff!!! It works! – works!! – works!!! — Glen, father

We enjoyed it immensely and read it for our family devotions.
— Jeannette, mother

What an incredible tool this book is! I found it absolutely packed with useful information. No doubt one of the best books and most enjoyable I've ever read.
— Kim, mother

It has been an answer to my prayers.
— Betty, mother

This book should be required reading for all families. — Hilary, mom

I wept as I began reading your book. I know God is going to use this book for total restoration in our family.
— Marty, mother

The stories had us roaring because it sounded just like our family.
— Family in Colorado

It is fun to hear the children remind each other, "Remember what Sarah said," "Don't forget what Stephen learned," "I don't think Grace would do that."
— Laura, mother

What a delightful book! I'm not sure what I was expecting but it was much more.
— Mother in Minnesota

WOW!!! I can tell you that I read your book in one sitting and I laughed so hard that my kids had to ask me to keep the noise down.
— Sue, mother

Making
Brothers and Sisters
Best Friends

How to Fight the GOOD Fight at Home!

Making Brothers and Sisters Best Friends

Best Friends

How to Fight the GOOD Fight at Home!

By Sarah, Stephen, and Grace Mally
Illustrated by Our Dad

Making Brothers and Sisters Best Friends
Copyright © 2006 by Sarah, Stephen, and Grace Mally

Published by
Tomorrow's Forefathers, Inc.
PO Box 11451
Cedar Rapids, Iowa 52410-1451

Production arrangements by
Winters Publishing
PO Box 501
Greensburg, Indiana 47240
800-457-3230

Cover design: Jeremy Fisher
Cover illustration: Harold Mally
Illustrations: Harold Mally

Fourth Printing (Revised edition) 2006
Printed in the United States of America

All Scripture references are from the King James Version.

Library of Congress Control Number: 2002093295
ISBN-10: 0-9719405-0-9
ISBN-13: 978-0-9719405-0-5

The following cartoons
demonstrate the need
for this book.

The Exciting Adventures of:

TABLE OF CONTENTS

We gratefully dedicate
this book to our parents,
Harold and Rebekah Mally.

We are best friends today because
of your godly example, wise teaching,
many prayers, and incredible
investment in our lives.
Thank you for training us up
in the way that we should go.
By the grace of God,
we shall not depart from it.

EACH CHAPTER CONTAINS:

- **A Section by Sarah**
  Insights from a firstborn's perspective

- **A Section by Stephen**
  Comments from a male and middle child's perspective

- **A Section by Grace**
  Thoughts and ideas from the youngest in the family

- **I'm Perplexed...**
  Common questions and answers

- **HIS Story Applied Today**
  Insights from a Bible story

- **A Self-Evaluation Quiz**

HOW TO USE THIS BOOK:

One suggestion that has been given to us by our proofreaders is to read this book aloud as a family. We'd like to pass this idea on to you. It strikes us as an excellent way to encourage the whole family and generate discussion, laughs, and family fellowship. In fact, we have now received many encouraging letters from families who have written to report many benefits from reading it aloud together.

Thank you! May the Lord bless your family.

Sarah, Stephen, and Grace

Home Sweet Home: In Crisis

Why Your Own Family is Often Your Biggest Struggle

SARAH'S SECTION

Why Your Own Family is Often Your Biggest Struggle

I was an only child until I was six years old. I really wanted a brother or sister, and I would pray everyday that God would give us a new baby. I assumed that once I had a brother or sister we would get along perfectly. It never crossed my mind that we might fight; I was sure that we would be best friends. But then one day God answered my prayer. I was thrilled to have a brother (and soon after a sister). It didn't take me long to learn of their amazing talents—they messed up my stuff, bothered me constantly, and displayed unbelievable amounts of energy. I soon learned that, although brothers and sisters really are a blessing, they often come in disguised packages.

A brother and sister were traveling in the back of a small station wagon on their way to Florida. The girl was nine years old and the boy was three. About five minutes down the road the arguing began. From the backseat their parents heard continually, "Don't poke me."

"Gimme my thtuffed aminal back!"

"Mom, he keeps bothering me!" The two children were crowded, uncomfortable, and easily annoyed. Finally, the two of them made an agreement.

"I THINK YOUR NEW SYSTEM IS GOING TO MAKE TRAVEL A LOT EASIER, DEAR."

"This half of the car is mine and this half is yours," they decided. "There is an invisible line down the middle."

"Now don't you touch my side," said the girl.

"K, an dif ith my thide. Thtay off!" came back the reply.

Things were peaceful until the little boy "accidentally" crossed his foot into enemy territory. "Mom, he touched my side!" was promptly heard and the debate continued ... all the way to Florida. I was this little girl and my brother, Stephen, was this little boy.

Do not be surprised if you have struggles with your brothers and sisters. It is a common problem for almost all families. However, *common* does not mean *acceptable*. Stephen, Grace, and I have been more and more concerned about this as we have noticed the way brothers and sisters often treat each other. Do not allow yourself to believe that it's okay for your relationship to remain substandard or that it cannot be improved. I can truly say that my brother and sister are my closest friends and great blessings in my life.

Be An Overcomer

It is not unusual that you have struggles, but it is extremely important that you deal with them properly. Struggles in life usually do not come at a convenient time; rather, they seem to come when we least expect them. They come in all different forms and in surprising ways. Our family is learning that it is important to see every obstacle as an opportunity. For example:

Sometimes you are helpless and the only solution is to be rescued. You can't do it by yourself.

One time our family was traveling late at night. This is not unusual. Our family seems to have a history of traveling late. I think that is because it takes SOME of us too long to pack. (You might be able to figure out who after completing this book.) It was about 10:00 P.M. and we were on our way to a homeschool conference. We thought it was a nice, peaceful, uneventful evening. Then all of a sudden we felt a jerk. Everyone sat up, opened their eyes, and looked around with frightened expressions. Dad quickly swerved to the side of the road and informed us of the good news. It was only a blowout. The bad news was that we were in the middle of nowhere—along the interstate in Indiana. Dad said, "Everyone get out of the van right away."

So there in the dark Mom and the three of us stood in the grass while Dad tried to put on the spare. Unfortunately, he could not get the jack underneath the van. (I guess SOME of us had packed too much.) After trying quite a few times, he finally decided that he would try to flag someone down to help. We were still standing along the road and praying while Dad was waving at every car that passed. No one stopped. More cars went by. Still no one stopped. It was getting late but we didn't have anything else we could do but wait. Then our faces brightened as we saw a car pull over and two young men get out to help us. They seemed to have a lot of experience and a lot of energy. It didn't take them long to lift up our van and get the jack underneath. After the spare tire was fixed, Dad explained to them that we sometimes get in situations where we can do nothing to help ourselves, and we need someone to come and rescue us.

"That's how it is when it comes to God," Dad continued. "We are trapped by sin and can do nothing to help ourselves. We need a rescuer. That's why we needed God to send His Son. When Jesus died on the cross, He did what we could not do for ourselves." He told the boys we were sorry there was nothing we could give them, but asked if we could at least pray for them. They said, "Yes," so Dad prayed, and then they left.

We were all relieved that our struggle was over and happily climbed back into our van, excited to continue on our way. But now we had a new problem. Dad turned the key and the car didn't start! We couldn't believe it. The lights had been on too long! Mom and the three of us climbed out of the van for the second time and the whole thing happened all over again. We started praying while Dad tried to flag someone else down. This time a man in a work truck pulled over. He jumped our van and it started. He had to leave in a hurry but we saw to it that he left with a tract. For the third time that night we climbed into our van ... this time to stay, and we made it safely to our destination.

Does your family have a flat tire right now? Are you on the side of the road? Did you have a blowout that shook the household and brought you to a stop? Maybe you don't have the right tools. But God does.

The obstacles involved in getting our car back on the road gave us the opportunity to witness, pray, demonstrate patience and endurance, and feel what it's like to be helpless. God doesn't allow difficulties unless He has a reason for them. Struggles are often the greatest chances for growing and ministering to others.

Problems are a normal part of life. Therefore, it is not surprising that you have struggles with your brothers and sisters. Your response will determine whether you will be defeated by these problems or overcome them. Victorious warriors are not defeated or discouraged by difficulties. Rather, they see them as a challenge. Our goal in this book is to share with you how you can fight the **good** fight by responding to family struggles in the right way.

You may ask, "But *why* is it so hard in my own family?"

Six Reasons for Family Conflict

1. False Concepts
Have you ever believed any of these things?
> *"My brother or sister is a problem in my life."*
> *"If I didn't have a brother/sister think how much easier my life would be."*
> *"Things are hopeless in our relationship."*
> *"The problem is their fault, not mine."*
> *"We get along as well as anybody else. I don't need to worry about this."*
> *"I'm just normal."*
> *"It's too late to do anything about our relationship now."*

These are lies that must be recognized, rejected, and replaced with truth. *"For though we walk in the flesh, we do not war after the flesh: (For the weapons of our warfare are not carnal, but mighty through God to the pulling down of strongholds:) Casting down imaginations and every high thing that exalteth itself against the knowledge of God, and bringing into captivity every thought to the obedience of Christ."* (II Cor. 10:3–5)

2. Bitterness

Many family problems are caused by offenses that lead to bitterness. We hurt others, sometimes intentionally and sometimes unintentionally, and we don't correct things. This damages their spirit toward us and causes bitterness. Also, when others hurt us, we do not respond in the right way. If there are offenses from the past that have never been cleared up, we cannot expect to maintain a good relationship in the present. We will explain this further in chapter four.

3. Higher Expectations of Our Family

We think we deserve more from our family. We want them to respect our time, space, and opinions. We expect the love and care that we see them show to other people. After all, we are their own sister (or brother); we deserve their love and service more than anyone else does. When they don't measure up to our expectations, we become angry and feel justified in cutting off the relationship. Then we often begin to seek approval from friends instead of our own family.

4. Lower Expectations of Ourselves

We tend to lower our expectations of ourselves when we are around our own family. We do not make the effort or take the time to consider their needs in the way we would think of other people's. After all, they are only our brothers and sisters. Our careless attitude is displayed by outward actions—we say things to them that we would be ashamed to say to others, we fail to express gratitude, we criticize, and we tease. In general, we make their life miserable and it doesn't even bother us.

In other words, we have **lower expectations** of ourselves, and **higher expectations** of them. Of course, this uncovers yet another problem. It is the other way around for them! As you can guess, this is a family self–destruct combination.

5. Distractions

If we are too busy to spend time with our families, we will not have a close relationship with them. Many distractions come along to occupy our time. These often keep us from the many important assignments God has for us, including our brothers and sisters. How can we expect to have a good relationship if we do not spend any time together? Some of these distractions are the television, the computer, the telephone, sports, video games, books, other friends, and busy schedules.

6. Hidden Enemy Influences
- From the beginning, Satan has tried to undermine and destroy God's plan. A godly family has much potential for the Lord. The enemy knows this and works very hard to destroy families. He has many lies, snares, and strategies. (I Pet. 5:8)
- The world is also working against us. We are surrounded by influences and teachings which do not encourage relationships in the family.
- Many young people strive to make friends, rather than concentrate on the family God has already given them. They think that it is not considered "cool" if you are nice to your brother or sister. Being best friends with your own family is not even considered a conceivable possibility. In fact, they think it's unheard of!

A little boy named Joey was told by his parents that they were having company for dinner. Since they didn't have enough room at the big table, they said he would have to sit at a little table with his brother and sister. When it was time for dinner, Joey's dad asked him to give thanks for the meal. Joey prayed, "O Lord, thank you for preparing a table before me in the presence of my enemies."

STEPHEN'S SECTION

I Can't Run That Far

I am the second oldest, the second youngest, and also the only boy. It's a good thing that I'm helping to write this book to give a male perspective.

Someone may ask the question, "I get along fine with my friends. Why can't I get along with my family?" If you, like others, have asked this, then congratulations for thinking of a great question!

Let me answer by giving you an illustration. When I am with my friends I am only running a sprint (a short race). Now, even though I might not be a very good runner, I can probably fool them and at least make it to the finish line. Why? Because I don't have very far to run. My friends will not know if I collapse right after I finish. When I am with my family, things are different. With them we are running a marathon. In the race of life, none of us are perfect runners. We all get tired, we all trip and fall, we all take breaks, and we all make mistakes. I might be able to fake it on a sprint, but I can't fake it on a marathon.

When I am with my friends, they think that I am easy to get along with (a very sensible thing to think). I would like to agree with them, but I know that in reality I am more careful what I say around them, more patient with their flaws, more flexible with their plans, and more cautious about how I act. For example, when I am with my friends and things don't go exactly as planned, I can tolerate that; I don't get frazzled or flare up. But with my family, I say what I think. In my family, I **do** care if things aren't going the way I was expecting, and I will notify them at my earliest convenience (not theirs!).

When I'm with my friends, they won't tell me what to do. I can sit down, rest, and have a good time. With my family, on the other hand, there always seems to be work to do. If I sit down to take a break—a much deserved break—a family member will certainly walk by and be excited to notice my availability. My friends see me on days that are going well, when the sun is shining and I'm happy and cheerful (or if I'm not, at least I pretend to be). My family sees me all the time, even on bad days when I'm sick, depressed, exhausted, stressed out, or suffering from a headache.

Since we are running the whole marathon of life with our family, we tend to have a lot of expectations of them. We are relying on them to help us through. We think that they should be more courteous to us at meals,

treat us with more respect, be more attentive to our needs, or at least not get mad about how we hold our fork. Since we are only on a sprint with our friends, we don't expect them to be perfect. They can ask us dumb questions or interrupt us when we are talking and it doesn't bother us that much. But with our family ... well, that's a different story.

Once Sarah, Grace, and I were going to a meeting that started at 5:00.

Chapter One: Home Sweet Home: In Crisis

Our family is often late because some of the people in our family take longer to get ready than others. There are five in our family. Three of *us* are fast and two of *them* are slow. (Names have not been listed to protect the guilty.) On this particular day, we decided that we would leave at 4:45. Sarah and I were ready on time and waiting in the car. But Grace was still flying around the house gathering together her large collection of assorted, unnecessary items. If this had happened at a friend's house, I probably would not have minded. I would have thought, "It's no big deal. We'll just be a little late." But in our own family, it is different. I expect everyone to be considerate of everyone else's schedule. Sarah and I have had experience with this, and we were trying to be creative. We started to sing a little song while we waited,

> *Be patient. Be patient.*
> *Don't be in such a hurry,*
> *If you get impatient, you only start to worry.*
> *Remember, remember, that God is patient, too*
> *And think of all the times when others have to wait for you!*

So, no problem, right? Well, unfortunately, there **was** a problem. Grace finally came (about 5:00) and we were still singing. You must understand that Grace, being the littlest, can get her feelings hurt easily. If someone in another family had been singing this song, she probably would have thought it was a funny joke, but since it was her own family, she took it personally. We didn't realize she felt this way until we arrived at our destination and Grace called home and told Mom she was really sad. She said, "Sarah and Stephen are being mean." From that incident we learned that showing patience is more than just singing a song. Actually, by singing the song, Sarah and I showed that we were not demonstrating patience. Instead, we were just irritating Grace by rubbing in the fact that she was late.

Another obvious point is that since we are running a marathon with our family, and only sprints with our friends, we are spending a lot more time with our siblings. After all, we see our family every day. Now, we may be defending ourselves in our mind, saying that we have a lot of good reasons why we can't get along with our siblings. I'm sure we could explain in detail why it is not our fault. But that's not the right attitude. We want to win the marathon and God has given us our families to help us. God doesn't want one of us to win; He wants the whole family to win. We have to learn that we aren't running *against* each other, but *with* each other.

If we only ran sprints with our family, we would be fine. But we are locked into a family marathon. Is there a remedy? That's what this book is about. Just think if you could finish the marathon and still be friends with your family—better yet, best friends!

Stephen's Definitions

Brother — A practically perfect person who helps his sisters learn character.

Book — A random selection of words compiled to make a point that some people may not like.

Expectations — An idea that you hope someone will do at a certain time, in a certain place, to a certain person, in order to benefit you in a certain way.

Patience — A character quality which children under five instinctively aim to develop in those around them.

Home — A place where you can say what you think, but no one listens.

Friends — People who usually have the same virtues, the same enemies, or the same faults.

Family trees — They seem to produce a variety of nuts.

GRACE'S SECTION

How It All Started

I was sitting in the car one day when Sarah said to me, "Grace, I have an idea. I think we should write a book to help brothers and sisters get along."

I thought, "Oh, boy! Here we go, another one of Sarah's big ideas!"

Sarah, Stephen, and I have all noticed that many brothers and sisters have damaged friendships. We agree that this is a huge problem. Everywhere we look, families seem to be having trouble. That is why we agreed to Sarah's idea of writing this book.

Actually, we shouldn't be surprised if it's hard to get along with our brothers and sisters, because Cain and Abel, the very first brothers that ever lived on this earth, didn't get along. They not only fought, but Cain actually killed Abel! Their fighting probably started when they were little.

The good news is that it doesn't have to be that way. God has the answers we need. You see, God is the One who has put us in families. This was His plan. He put each one of us in a family that is just right for us. Our brothers and sisters are blessings and gifts from the Lord.

Since We Are Not Perfect...

Obviously, kids aren't perfect like grown-ups are (ha ha ha). Therefore, we don't always get along perfectly. And since we know our brothers and sisters better than we know anyone else, that makes it more challenging to get along with them.

For example, I am very relaxed around Sarah and Stephen because I know them so well. As a result, I am not "on guard" most of the time and can easily become careless in my actions, attitudes, and words. I am not as careful to do what is right. After all, they already know that I have a lot of faults; I don't need to worry about my reputation when I'm with them.

Whenever people are careless and respond without thinking, it leads to problems. A few years ago my dad had gallbladder surgery. The night after his surgery he was very sore. He had a hard time getting from the chair to the bed. Mom was helping him so he wouldn't pull or stretch anything. Very slowly he crawled into bed, carefully lay down, and went to sleep.

In the middle of the night ... Ring! Ring! The phone rang, and, boy,

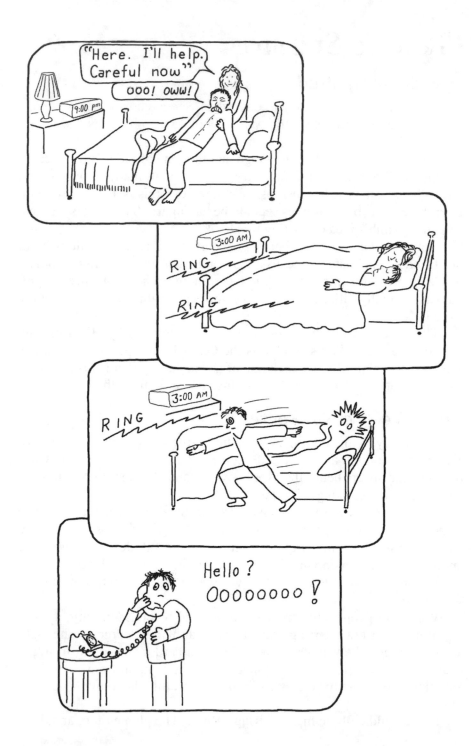

was my mom surprised when she saw Dad spring out of bed and run to get the phone. OUCH! I think my dad was a little surprised, too. He was so sound asleep that he had forgotten about everything until he got to the phone ... then he remembered the surgery.

Dad was trying to be really cautious before he went to bed, but then when something unexpected happened, he forgot all about being "on guard." Ouch! That hurt! In the same way, since we are not always "on guard" in our family, it is easy for problems to arise.

Learning to Have Jesus' Responses

One time when I was about three years old, I was having a great time playing at the park. Right in the middle of my fun, Sarah came to me and said it was time to go home. I didn't want to go home at all. I wanted to stay and play at the park all day! The right response would have been for me to submit to Sarah and to do what she wanted. Instead, my "automatic response" caused trouble for me (and for her). I ran away from her, hid in the slide, and tried to think of any possible way to stay longer at the park. After all, I thought, "Sarah is not my mother." Finally, it took a mutual effort between Stephen and Sarah to drag me home. Actually, I don't remember this story but Stephen and Sarah have told it to me many times. They say they remember it well, because it happened every time they took me to the park!

Excuses...

1. Have you noticed that sometimes brothers and sisters don't even try to get along? Several girls I know often complain about their brothers and sisters. They tell me:

   - "My brother is so mean to me."
   - "I hate it when my sister baby-sits me."
   - "My siblings are the biggest pests in the world."

   They don't seem to care about this relationship, and definitely are not planning to take any steps to correct things.

2. Then there are some who just make excuses. They think:

   - "Well, no one gets along with their brothers and sisters, so why should I?"
   - "Get along with them? That is impossible!"
   - "They don't like me, so I'm not going to worry about it."
   - "We're not as bad as *that family*!"

3. Other people actually do **want** to improve but they don't take any **action**. They may recognize the problem, but are always too lazy to do anything about it. Sometimes I realize, "Well, I could get along with Sarah better in this way," or "Stephen and I could handle this situation better," but I just think about it and don't do anything.

Do any of these examples fit your family? Then continue reading this book. Also, remember that God is on our side, and although this book won't give you all the help and answers you need, the Bible will.

"There hath no temptation taken you but such as is common to man: but God is faithful, who will not suffer you to be tempted above that ye are able; but will with the temptation also make a way to escape, that ye may be able to bear it." (I Cor. 10:13)

SARAH'S SECTION

The Incredible Influence of a Godly Family

This is the exciting part of this chapter! Godly families have incredible influence. The benefits to the Kingdom of God will be tremendous if we are willing to seek His best in this area. Few people realize how much influence they have on those around them. John 13:35 says, *"By this shall all men know that ye are My disciples, if ye have love one to another."*

Imagine the things you normally see in a grocery store. I often see parents yelling at their kids, unhappy faces, anger, teasing, selfishness, and brothers and sisters who are fighting and arguing. I remember one time sitting in our car, in a parking lot, waiting for Stephen. I was trying to study but was very distracted by the people in the van next to me. I couldn't see into it very well, but I could hear screaming and yelling. Needless to say, the family in that van was not getting along. They were literally screaming at each other in intense anger. I couldn't believe what I was hearing. It is sad that this is what many people are used to and even expect. But think of what a contrast families will be who show the humility, kindness, and love that Jesus commands—especially if they show it even to their own *brothers and sisters!*

We are often surprised at how much people watch our family. They make comments about us when we didn't even think they were noticing. This is a constant reminder that we are representing the Lord Jesus Christ everywhere we go. People are just not used to seeing families that get along. I remember one time our family did a presentation at a church. Afterwards, a lady came up to talk to me. Instead of saying something about our music or the presentation, she said, "I wanted to tell you how impressed I was by the way you and your sister got along together." I was surprised. I didn't think we had done anything special. My internal reaction was, "Even if we do not get along well at home, do you think we'd fight **in public**?? ... let alone **on stage**??" Nevertheless, that was what impressed her. We are definitely not a perfect family (you will find that out by reading this book!), but we want you to realize that families who are trying to do what is right *will* be noticed.

Wherever you go, you, as a strong, loving family, will be so rare that you will stand out brightly. Do not underestimate the importance of this testimony. By obeying the Lord in your relationship with your family, you will be lifting up a banner for the glory of the Lord Jesus Christ that will be seen by many. This godly strategy is "fighting the good fight."

"When the enemy shall come in like a flood, the Spirit of the Lord shall lift up a standard against him." (Is. 59:19b)

Application

- **Accept** God's design for your family. God is the One who has given you the family that you have. His ways are perfect and He has a purpose for what He does. If you are upset about a certain aspect of your family (such as who your brothers and sisters are, how many you have, or your birth order), you are actually upset at God. *"Nay but, O man, who art thou that repliest against God? Shall the things formed say to him that formed it, Why hast thou made me thus? Hath not the potter power over the clay?"* (Rom. 9:20-21a)

- **Thank** God for your family, for each of your brothers and sisters, and specifically for anything about your family which you do not like. It is essential that you do this if you want to successfully apply the other things in this book. *"In every thing give thanks: for this is the will of God in Christ Jesus concerning you."* (I Thess. 5:18)

- **Choose** now that you want to do whatever it takes to establish a godly, strong, edifying relationship with each of your brothers and sisters. Just reading a book will not fix things in your family. It is up to you to choose that you will obey the Lord and seek His best, whatever the cost.

This is not just for your sake, not just for their sake, not just for your parents' sake, but for the glory of the Lord, for the defeat of the enemy, and for a dynamic testimony to the lives of everyone with whom you come in contact! Godly families are few and far between in this *"crooked and perverse generation"* (Phil. 2:15) in which brothers and sisters are looked upon as irritations, unsolvable problems, and blemishes in your life.

I'M PERPLEXED...

Question: What if my brothers and sisters "don't care" about our relationship?

Answer: First of all, it is probably not true that they "don't care" about your relationship. They may *think* they don't care, *say* they don't care, *pretend* they don't care, or *want you to think* they don't care, but really, they *do* desire your friendship. Do not be discouraged. It will mean a lot to your brother or sister that **you do care**. Your effort will not be in vain.

Secondly, **you** are the key to the solution. It usually only takes one person to clear up a conflict. If one person is willing to obey the Lord, amazing things can happen. It is not your responsibility to force them to work things out; it is your responsibility to be sure that **you** are obedient to the Lord and then to leave the results to Him. *"For God is not unrighteous to forget your work and labour of love, which ye have showed toward His name, in that ye have ministered to the saints, and do minister."* (Heb. 6:10)

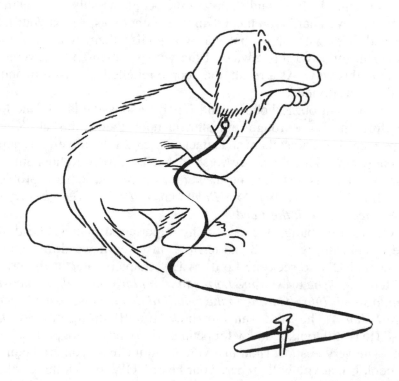

HIS STORY APPLIED TODAY

The Impact of One Decision

Life would be a lot easier if we could just make wise decisions all the time. Have you thought about how amazing it would be if we could be like King Solomon, the wisest man who ever lived? I have. But did you know that Solomon had a son named Rehoboam who made an extremely foolish decision?

When Solomon died, all of Israel gathered together to make Rehoboam king. The people approached him with a question. They said, "Your father put a heavy yoke on us, but now, lighten the harsh labor and make things easier for us. We will then serve you." Rehoboam answered, "Give me three days to decide and then I will tell you my decision."

In the meantime, Rehoboam wanted to get some advice. First of all, he talked to the elders, the old men who had served with his father. They told him he should answer favorably and gently to the people.

But King Rehoboam rejected the wise advice of the older men and went to talk to his friends that he had grown up with. They gave him the opposite counsel. They said, "Answer the people harshly. Tell them that you will be even harder on them than your father was — that your father punished them with whips but you will punish them with scorpions." Rehoboam followed this advice of the younger men and answered the people in this way. As a result, the people rebelled against him and the kingdom was divided.

As life went on, Rehoboam and Judah forsook the law of the Lord. Therefore, the Lord brought punishment upon them; Shishak, King of Egypt, came up against them and attacked them. Why did all this happen to Rehoboam? There is a key verse that tells us why Rehoboam made these foolish decisions. It is the answer to why he had so many problems. (Read II Chronicles 12:14) *"And Rehoboam did evil because he **prepared not his heart to seek the Lord**."*

We are still young. We have many important decisions ahead of us. Like Rehoboam, we will make terrible mistakes if we do not prepare our hearts NOW to seek the Lord. A few chapters later in II Chr. 16:9 God tells us, *"The eyes of the Lord run to and fro throughout the whole earth to show Himself strong in the behalf of them whose heart is perfect toward Him."* The Lord wants to show Himself strong in each of our lives. He is still looking today for people whose hearts are perfect before Him. The very best decision that you could make as you are beginning this book is that you will prepare your heart NOW to seek the Lord.

Self-Evaluation Quiz 1

1. **My brother/sister is my...**
   - ❑ Pet.
   - ❑ Slave.
   - ❑ Enemy.
   - ❑ Biggest problem in life.
   - ☒ Best friend.

2. **When I'm with my brother/sister I...**
   - ❑ Yawn.
   - ❑ Contact the local pest control.
   - ☒ Enjoy our time together.
   - ❑ Look forward to heaven.
   - ❑ Ignore them.

3. **I pray specifically for my brother/sister...**
   - ❑ Everyday.
   - ☒ Not very much.
   - ❑ Only at mealtimes.
   - ❑ When they are sick.

4. **I tend to respond to family struggles by...**
   - ☒ Ignoring the problem.
   - ☒ Blaming others.
   - ❑ Sleeping through them.
   - ❑ Escaping to the telephone or the television.
   - ❑ Going to the Bible.
   - ☒ Trying to forget about them.

5. **When I'm in the middle of a busy project, and my brother comes in to annoy me, my usual response is...**
   - ❑ To make a big sign which says, "DO NOT DISTURB!" and tape it to my shirt.
   - ☒ To say, "You can have 45 seconds to talk to me. On your mark, get set, go."
   - ☒ To explain to my brother what I am doing and begin to delegate work.
   - ☒ To remember that my brother is more important than my project, and determine how I can encourage him.
   - ❑ To ask him to find out the daily news for me, the weather forecast, the gas prices, and how much milk we have left.

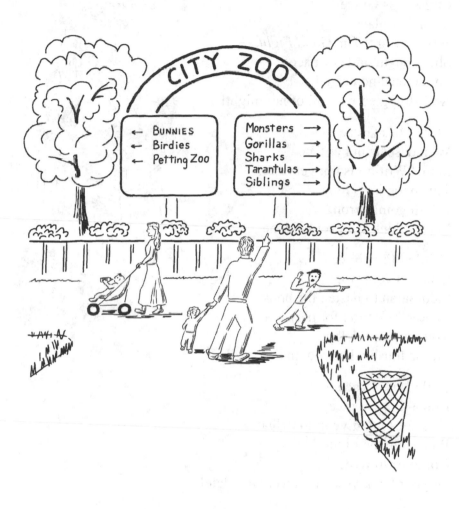

Little Miss Grace

Little Miss Grace
Sat in her place
Writing *Fight The Good Fight.*
She thought and she paced
She wrote and erased
And struggled with all of her might!

Little Miss Grace
With despair in her face
Said, "Writing is not very fun.
This book is so long
It's all going wrong
I don't think I'll ever be done."

"Little Miss Grace
Quicken your pace,"
Said Sarah to hasten the book.
"There's no time for play,
You must not delay,
Please finish what you undertook."

Little Miss Grace
Run a diligent race
You must not give in to defeat.
Work into the night
Continue to write
Or your book you will never complete!

Little Miss Grace
Has delight in her face
"I'm finished! I'm finished," she said.
"You say, I'm not done?
That was just chapter one?
I think that I'll just go to bed!"

CHAPTER TWO

The Chance Of A Lifetime

Your Life Work Starts in Your Family

SARAH'S SECTION

Your Life Work Starts in Your Family

The attitude of many Christians is, "I want to do something great for the Lord. I want to make my life count for Christ. Lord, send me anywhere."

Suppose a servant comes to a king and says, "I am committed to you. I am your loyal servant. I will be faithful to you, no matter what. You can count on me. Just give me an assignment."

The king thinks for a minute and says, "Would you please take this message and deliver it to my knight?"

The servant replies, "What? You just want me to deliver a message? I wanted to do something great for you. I thought you would send me to battle so I could perform some brave and gallant deed for the service and honor of the king." What would the king think of a servant like that? He probably would not have a very high opinion of him anymore. He would have no confidence in him, and definitely would not choose him for the important assignments.

Sometimes I wonder if we appear this way to God. The Lord has asked us to be faithful in the little things. Do we dare ask to do great things for God if we neglect to obey Him in the small things? No, our first step is to obey Him in the things He has already asked us to do. Jesus commanded His disciples to be witnesses first in Jerusalem, then in Judea, then Samaria, and finally, to the uttermost part of the earth. In the same way, the very first place God sends each one of us is to our own families. It is easy to treat our relationship with our brothers and sisters as unimportant, but it's not unimportant in God's eyes.

The Lord taught me a lesson about the importance of little things once when our family was in Florida. We were combining a series of harp programs with a family vacation. My brother, sister, and I each play the harp and my grandparents had arranged a concert for us at a Christian conference. Many people came to our program and we had a great response. I was very excited about this ministry opportunity.

Soon after that, as we traveled through Florida, my dad mentioned that we were stopping to visit an older lady who was a friend of my grandmother. As we arrived at her mobile home, Dad said, "I think we should take the harps in to play for her."

With surprise I said, "Take the harps in? Here?" Taking the harps in meant unloading everything that was on top of them and our van was very full. I knew it would be a major ordeal to get the harps up the steps, in the house, back out, down the steps, and into the van underneath the luggage again. Besides, we were in a hurry to get to our destination that evening. I said, "Dad, how about if we just bring the little harp inside and leave the big one in the van?"

But Dad replied, "No, I think we should bring them both in." We moved the harps into her living room and began to play some music for her. I immediately realized that it was worth the effort. This lady had no family and only a few friends. She rarely had the chance to go anywhere—even to church. Therefore, our harp music, which I considered insignificant, was extremely meaningful to her. After playing some hymns and talking with her for awhile, we continued on our way. As we climbed back into the van, the Lord convicted me of my wrong attitude. I had been so willing and excited to play for the big crowd at the conference, but I thought it was too much work to play for this lady. Then I remembered that in Scripture the Lord tells us how concerned He is about widows and orphans. I began to think that perhaps God saw this "harp concert" for one lady as a more important ministry than the one that I thought was so big. The Lord reminded me that sometimes the things that seem big in my eyes are little to Him, and the things that seem little to me are big to Him. This includes our brothers and sisters.

So, our goal is to obey the Lord by doing the small things. How can we apply this in our family? As we think of ways to minister to our brothers and sisters, we may be excited about being a leader or a good example or a teacher to the younger ones. Those things are good, but they do not come first.

Remember the servant who came to the king and wanted to do something important? That is a common attitude. People naturally desire to be great but there is an unexpected quality of greatness that is quite uncommon. We all tend to overlook and ignore it. Do you know what it is?

The unexpected quality is being a servant. Even Jesus came, not to be served, but to serve. Matt. 23:11-12 says, *"But he that is greatest among you shall be your servant. And whosoever shall exalt himself shall be abased and he that shall humble himself shall be exalted."* (Also read Luke 22:24-27 and Mark 10:42-45.) When Jesus washed His disciples' feet, He told them, *"Ye call Me Master and Lord: and ye say well; for so I am. If I then, your Lord and Master have washed your feet: ye also ought to wash one another's feet."* (See John 13:14 and Phil. 2:7)

The world's thinking is, "If you want to be a leader, make yourself

great." But that is not God's thinking. God tells us that if we want to be great, we should humble ourselves and let God exalt us. Proverbs 22:4 says, *"By humility and the fear of the Lord are riches, honor, and life."* As we seek to be godly leaders in our families, our very first assignment is to learn what seems like the opposite. Be a servant; look for opportunities to humble yourself and unselfishly serve others.

Characteristics of a True Servant

A true servant:
- ❑ Knows that all assignments are actually from God
- ❑ Will be quick to volunteer
- ❑ Considers his assignment important
- ❑ Takes orders
- ❑ Does not desire to have authority
- ❑ Will do what others do not or will not do
- ❑ Enjoys meeting needs

- ❑ Doesn't need recognition
- ❑ Will voluntarily serve without pay
- ❑ Doesn't seek higher status
- ❑ Will do more than is required
- ❑ Does not have his own selfish ambitions
- ❑ Will serve anyone—even those whom others don't like to serve
- ❑ Is willing to be treated like a servant
- ❑ Does not seek the "big" and "important" assignments
- ❑ Will serve with a joyful attitude
- ❑ Will put his whole heart into each task
- ❑ Thinks of others before himself
- ❑ Desires that his master receives the credit
- ❑ Desires that God receives the glory

God has given to each of us the perfect place to learn to be a servant—at home! Everyday there are many opportunities for us to serve our parents and brothers and sisters. Actually, home is the most difficult place to serve, so I think that if we learn to be a servant in our own family, we will be able to be a servant anywhere. We must not reject this first assignment from the Lord by asking for a better one.

The key to having a servant's attitude is to remember that we are ultimately not serving others; we are serving the Lord. *"And whatsoever ye do, do it heartily, as to the Lord, and not unto men; Knowing that of the Lord ye shall receive the reward of the inheritance; for ye serve the Lord Christ."* (Col. 3:23-24)

I remember one time when the Lord gave me a lesson in being a servant. I was at a Christian conference center, taking some classes in music and in teaching children. I had a break for four days and needed to return home because I had a lot of "important" things to do. I had a girls' discipleship group to lead, a harp job, a testimony to give at a luncheon, and various other things. It wasn't wrong that I returned home to do those things, but I realized later that my attitude had been wrong. I had been considering my work more "important" than that of my friends, who remained at the center to work in the kitchen and clean during those four days. The Lord was going to deal with this prideful attitude.

You see, things didn't go quite as I had planned. As soon as I arrived home, I came down with the flu and I was unable to do most of my "important" things. The only thing on my list that I **was** able to do was to make it to the luncheon. Guess what the speaker was talking about? He was explaining how God uses those who are humble and who consider themselves to be the least. I was beginning to understand what the Lord was teaching me. But that wasn't the end of my lesson. When I returned to the center, I was still sick, so my roommate took notes for me. She came back after the first evening and said, "The speaker tonight talked about how the Lord is looking for people who are willing to serve, who don't want the important jobs, but are anxious to put others first and just be a servant."

I was thinking, "Lord, I get Your point!"

God's Training Program

We serve a powerful God who is working in our lives in many ways. This next little story is just one example of a time that God was fitting details together in my life. We are often unaware of the way God is working behind the scenes.

One day I was planning Bright Lights for the following week. (Bright Lights is a discipleship group that I lead for younger girls.) I didn't have things planned yet, but it seemed that it would be a good week to go to a nursing home. We had just been talking about having ministry in Bright Lights and it had been over a year since we had ministered at a nursing home. I felt impressed that this was the right thing to do, but I didn't know which nursing home we should go to, or even if we could arrange one on this late notice.

I called one place that had been suggested to me, but they told me they plan everything at least a month in advance. I was wondering what to do. There are plenty of nursing homes, but I had no idea which one to call. I was praying and thinking about it when ... the phone rang.

My dad answered it and the lady said, "Hello, I'm calling from the Cottage Grove Place" (a nursing home near us). "I don't really know why I'm calling, but someone gave me your name and phone number, and it's been sitting on my desk for several weeks. I'm finally getting around to calling. I think it has something to do with a presentation someone was suggesting that you could do for us ..."

We've never received a call like that before, and she called at the very time I was looking for a nursing home! God's timing is amazing! Of course we said yes to the lady on the phone. All the details worked out, the presentation went well, and we were able to share with others how God's power had been demonstrated in this little incident.

Our Heavenly Father is personally concerned about His children. He is working in even the little details of our life to mold us to the image of His Son, Jesus Christ. (Rom. 8:28-29) Our Father is more concerned about our inward character than our outward achievement. He has a specialized training program for each of us. This training program begins at home. God's classes come in many unexpected ways, at unexpected times, in unexpected locations, and often through unexpected people—like brothers and sisters. In fact, brothers and sisters seem to be some of the most common "professors" in God's University. He is not only creative with His choice of teachers but also with His assignments and projects. Because we do not know the future, we often do not understand what God is doing. It takes faith to believe that His ways are perfect and that the family we are in is part of God's specialized program for us. If we cooperate with His training program we will be ready and prepared for the exciting future He has in store for us.

For example, God was preparing David for the very important assignment of being the king of Israel. His training program was certainly not a traditional one. In preparation for being the shepherd of the people of Israel, the Lord gave David the job of protecting, feeding, and leading his father's sheep. Apparently, this was a task often delegated to younger family members. There were many other stages of David's intense training program—fighting a giant, waiting, leading the king's army into battle, waiting, being chased by Saul, waiting, living in the wilderness, waiting, writing songs, waiting, and more waiting. He was waiting for God to accomplish His purposes. Some events in David's training made him famous and respected, but actually none were more important than the lowly job of protecting the sheep. That's where he started.

Likewise, Joseph's training program was not what he would have chosen. It included losing his mother, being sold by his brothers, being a slave in a foreign country, and spending years in prison. Yet Joseph was faithful. He passed his tests and the Lord exalted him to be ruler over the nation of Egypt.

We often hear about Amy Carmichael's ministry in India, but her ministry didn't begin on the mission field. It began at home. She diligently helped her mother with the younger children. She taught two of her sisters while they were too ill to attend school. Right at home, she began to hold meetings for children from her neighborhood.

Similarly, Corrie ten Boom demonstrated faithfulness to the Lord by having ministry at home. During World War II she protected many Jews, but long before the war started she was busy taking care of invalids and the homeless. She helped to care for three elderly aunts, for orphan children, and for the mentally retarded. She welcomed foster children into her home, and she initiated a ministry with girls by beginning a girls' club.

The well-known missionary to China, Hudson Taylor, is another example of one who began his ministry at home. While he was still at home, preparing for China, he handed out tracts with his younger sister, taught Sunday School, and visited the poor and sick.

The ministry that you have now at home will be excellent preparation and training for the future ministry God has for you. It has been said that if you can learn to get along with each member of your family, you will be able to get along with anyone in the world. I'm not saying that this training program is easy. David's and Joseph's were not easy. Little assignments can be difficult but the rewards will be worth every effort. Matthew 25:21 says, *"Well done, thou good and faithful servant: thou hast been faithful over a few things, I will make thee ruler over many things: enter thou into the joy of thy Lord."* The Lord will bless our little home ministries by giving us greater ministry. Right now it is our responsibility to be faithful in the "little" things. Do not underestimate the importance of this assignment. One day the King shall say, *"Verily I say unto you, Inasmuch as ye have done it unto one of the least of these My brethren, ye have done it unto Me."* (Matt. 25:40)

STEPHEN'S SECTION

Ask Yourself the Right Questions

After reading chapter one you may agree that you have a problem. (Maybe even several problems, some younger than you and some older.) Don't panic! The rest of the book is about how to solve those problems. The main point that we want you to understand in this chapter is that God's big assignments start with little ones, and God's training begins with learning how to be best friends at home.

Instead of asking yourself the question, "How can I persuade my brothers and sisters to treat me better?" I encourage you to try a new perspective. Ask yourself the questions, "How can I help them? What opportunities has the Lord given me to encourage or teach them?" Now as you begin to look for ways to minister to them, let me warn you, the best way to do this is not to stand on your soap box and start preaching,

"YOU SINNERS, REPENT FROM DOING WRONG THINGS TO YOUR BROTHER!" You might lose your audience. Be a learner from the big ones, a teacher to the little ones, and a servant of all. Don't be a boss or a know-it-all.

I have learned that God wants me to serve my family, not only for their benefit, but for my own benefit as well. The Lord is using these family experiences to teach me and prepare me for my future. For instance, when Grandma Mally was getting older she came to stay with us for awhile. We learned a lot from Grandma, but sometimes in ways we wouldn't have chosen. Because Grandma couldn't see or walk very well, the Lord gave me the opportunity to learn to be a servant. Everybody else in our family could take care of themselves, but Grandma needed help, and we had to prepare and serve all of Grandma's food.

The Fruit and the Fall

Grace and I will always remember the time that Grandma decided to get something for herself to eat. Grace, Grandma, and I were home alone. Grandma thought that she was baby-sitting us, so Grace and I didn't tell her that we were actually baby-sitting her. Later that evening, when I was playing Legos downstairs with Grace, we heard a strange noise from upstairs. It sounded like someone walking around very fast. We looked at each other with puzzled expressions. "Who could that be?" "Grandma can't walk very well, so it must be a robber!" we whispered.

Our curiosity overcame our fear and we cautiously crept up the stairs. As we were nearing the top, we heard another strange noise—the refrigerator door opening and closing. I guess the robber got hungry while robbing our house. As we continued on our dangerous mission, I led the way because Grace was scared. We reached the top of the stairs only to be startled by yet another strange noise: a loud bang! We ran into the kitchen and saw the robber!

"Wait, that's not a robber—it's Grandma!" She was sitting on the floor with a peach in her hand.

Apparently, this is what had happened ... Grandma wanted to eat some fruit and decided to undertake her project single-handedly. She got up (without her walker) and walked or stumbled into the kitchen. But she had to sort of run to keep her balance. She got her snack successfully, but then fell with a crash. Grace and I weren't sure what to do. We tried to help her up, but she kept falling back to the floor. After trying several times, we realized that she was too heavy for us. Now what? Then Grandma had another idea. She decided not to get up at all, but to slide across the kitchen floor and into the living room—all the way to the couch. Now we had the problem of getting her onto the couch. Grace and I got into position ... 1, 2, 3, push! After about three tries, we finally got her on the couch. So when Mom and Dad returned home, there she was sitting contentedly, pretending that nothing had happened.

God taught me a lot through my grandma. I learned to listen to the same stories over and over, to be gentle and resourceful, and to be willing to help the elderly. God has put a mission field right before us. We need to be understanding and encouraging to our siblings, parents, and grandparents. When we are ten, twelve, or sixteen years old, we may not have the opportunity to be a missionary to Africa, but we can fulfill

the ministry that God wants us to do right now, right here. *"He that is faithful in that which is least is faithful also in much."* (Luke 16:10)

Stephen's Definitions

Slave — Synonym for "son."

Perplexed — One sister who must make one left turn.

Confused — Two sisters who must make two left turns.

Disaster — When two lost sisters, who insist they have made two right turns, call home for directions, and no one is home but their mother!

Vacation — When you travel for days to get your picture taken next to your car.

Important — A false idea we have about ourselves.

GRACE'S SECTION

That's Too Hard

My grandma was in the car with a little girl. As the girl looked out the window, she saw a telephone pole and exclaimed, "I love Jesus so much, I think I could climb right up to the top of that telephone pole!"

"Well, you know," Grandma said, "I don't think Jesus would want you to climb the telephone pole, but I know something Jesus does want you to do."

"What?" asked the little girl eagerly.

My grandma answered, "I think He wants you to be nice to your brother."

"Oh, that's too hard!" the little girl said.

If you consider getting along with your family to be impossible, then your whole future is not off to a very good start! If you can't get along with your family, how will you be able to maintain good relationships with others later on?

Even if No One Notices...

As Sarah said, it is easy to find ourselves wanting to do the "big" things for God—the things everyone notices. One of the reasons for this is we want people to think well of us. I find myself wondering what people think of me so much more than I should! But it doesn't matter what anyone thinks of us, except God. And God is pleased when we are willing to do the "little" things like doing the dishes, taking out the garbage, and being kind to our brothers and sisters. Our home is the most important place for us to be encouraging, helpful, understanding, gentle, and patient, even though no one may notice. Have you ever thought that maybe God is more pleased with these things, than if we play our musical instrument at church, or say something in front of a group, or put money in the offering plate?

Try a New Perspective

Some days seem to be disasters. Do you ever have a day at your house where everything is going wrong? Does it ever seem like a big, sticky mess? It's on those days that you feel like throwing this book into the garbage and your siblings in the recycling bin. We've had days like that in our family.

One time, my mom was exhausted. She had been very busy all day and had just arrived home. Now all she felt like doing was getting a snack and taking a relaxing, hot, luxurious bath. No work, nothing to worry about, just take a bath, and then go to bed. Is your mom ever like that?

As she was fixing her snack, she went into the closet to get some honey. We have a lot of honey because we bake lots of bread. We keep it in a big, five-gallon bucket. Mom must have been overly tired, because somehow the container slipped and 60 pounds of honey spilled on our closet floor. And as you can guess, it soon escaped from the closet into the next room. Now Mom was exhausted, tired, and stuck to the closet floor. What a sticky mess! Too bad we didn't have a pet bear! Now Mom really wanted a bath.

On some days in our family it seems like everything is just one big, sticky mess! But is it really a disaster? Maybe we need a new perspective! Is it a disaster, or is God training you in a creative way? Is it just another family problem, or is it a special assignment from God? Is it a tragedy, or is it a new opportunity to learn? Sometimes God's assignments seem huge, but the rewards are even bigger!

I'M PERPLEXED...

Question: What if my brother and sister don't respond to my efforts?

Answer: Consider how the Lord has worked in your life. Have you always responded immediately or has He had to be patient with you? Many times it has taken me a long time to learn the lessons that God was trying to teach me. We ought to treat others the way He has treated us.

Have you ever seen a four-year-old with a seed to plant? They eagerly plant it in the ground, cover it with dirt, and sprinkle it with water. A few minutes later they return to see if it has grown, but they are disappointed to see nothing at all. The next morning they wake up with excitement and quickly run outside to look at their flower. "Surely it has grown by now," they think. They do not understand that they still have a long time to wait.

God relates our work on earth to sowing and reaping. We sow now but the fruit rarely comes right away. We may have to wait for years before we see all the fruit of our labor. Some fruit will not be known until eternity. But *"let us not be weary in well doing: for in due season we shall reap, if we faint not. As we have therefore opportunity, let us do good unto all men, especially unto them who are of the household of faith."* (Gal. 6:9-10) We, however, are often like four-year-olds expecting to see the fruit immediately.

Actually, you really don't need to worry about this question of how others respond to our efforts. We are serving the Lord and not man. Our goal is to please the Lord even if no one else notices or cares or responds. God is pleased and that is enough.

HIS STORY APPLIED TODAY

Little Brothers Are So Much Work

"Will you please watch your little brother? I need to go on some errands." Does this sound familiar to you? Do you ever feel like your parents' full-time, unpaid baby-sitter?

Many centuries ago there was a young lady who was asked to watch her little baby brother. I don't know how this young lady felt about this, but I do know that this was more than an ordinary baby-sitting job. The girl knew this, too. She recognized that her brother could lose his life if she was found out. Perhaps she was afraid. Maybe she was bored with this job and wanted to do something else. Who knows? But whether she felt like it or not, she was faithful with her task.

This girl's name was Miriam. Her brother was in a little basket floating in the river. She could not hold her baby brother. All she could do was watch the basket. Soon she found out that she was not the only one watching the basket. Pharaoh's daughter also noticed it, and upon opening it, she found the baby Moses. Miriam continued to be faithful with her baby-sitting assignment. She quickly came up with a plan for the baby to be nursed. Can you imagine how Miriam felt as she ran to get her own mother to nurse her own brother? Miriam was committed to her one little assignment: baby-sitting her brother. Her faithfulness changed the course of history. Moses became one of the greatest leaders the world has ever known. The Lord chose Moses to be the one who would deliver His people from slavery in Egypt and record the first five books of the Bible. So next time you are asked to baby-sit, remember Miriam and her baby-sitting job. Only God knows how our obedience will influence the world. (Ex. 2:1-9)

"And whatsoever ye do, do it heartily, as to the Lord, and not unto men." (Col. 3:23)

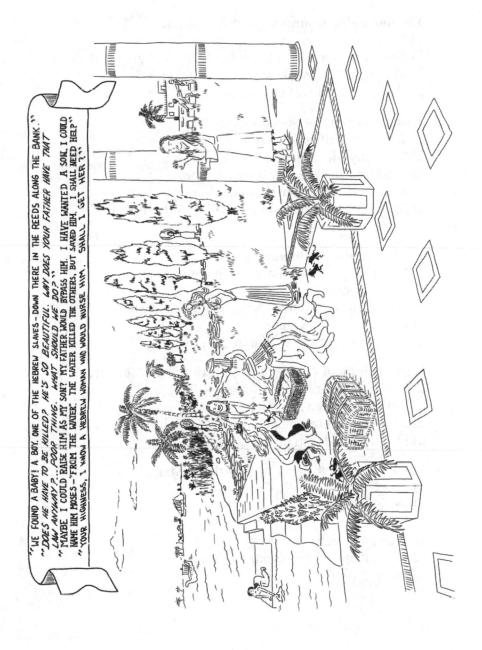

Self-Evaluation Quiz 2

1. **The more I'm around my brother/sister...**
   - ❑ The more I enjoy my teddy bear.
   - ❑ The more I wonder if it's possible to like being with them.
   - ❑ The more I can relate to my cat and dog.
   - ☒ The more I learn of God's plan for my life.

2. **I think my brother/sister's job is to...**
   - ☒ Think of creative ways to bug me.
   - ☒ Make my life difficult.
   - ☒ Teach me character by bothering me.
   - ☒ Add a special dimension to my life.
   - ❑ Spy on me and report to the FBI (Family Bureau of Investigation).

3. **For me, ministry at home is...**
   - ❑ Like trying to hand out tracts in a war zone.
   - ☒ A new concept.
   - ❑ A goal equivalent to climbing Mount Everest.
   - ❑ An exercise in patience.
   - ❑ An activity similar to lion training.

4. **When I think of God's "Training Program" for me...**
   - ❑ I see how things in my life fit together.
   - ☒ I'm afraid to see my report card.
   - ❑ I can sympathize with David and Joseph.
   - ☒ I wish I could start all over.

5. **I look for ways to serve my brother/sister...**
   - ❑ Everyday.
   - ☒ Once in a while.
   - ❑ Not ever.
   - ❑ When they serve me.
   - ❑ When they call me, "Your Highness."
   - ❑ I will ... later.

6. **When I find all my brother/sister's junk on my bed, my response is to...**
   - ☑ Remember that I am only a servant and do what a servant would do.
   - ❑ Sleep on it so they feel guilty when I have to go to the chiropractor.
   - ❑ Move it all onto their bed.
   - ❑ Take pictures of it and use it for my upcoming report on recycling.
   - ❑ Send them a parking ticket.

CHAPTER THREE

Skunks and Mothballs

Looking at the Future Picture

SEEING THE WHOLE PICTURE

SARAH'S SECTION

Looking at the Future Picture

- "I don't really care about my relationship with my brother or sister."
- "I have my friends. They have theirs. We like it that way."
- "We're only going to be together for a few more years anyway."
- "We're fine as long as we ignore each other."
- "Just avoiding each other is what works for us."
- "I have enough problems in my life. I don't need to be concerned about this one."
- "We never talk, but at least we don't fight."

If any of these statements reflect the way you feel, then I encourage you to step back and look at the bigger picture—the future picture. Many people make decisions based on what is the easiest or most fun right here and right now, but one who has faith understands that God has a bigger program. Think for a moment. What is God's goal in creating the family? God desires godly generations. From the beginning of history His purpose has been to raise up many generations of godly families.

Genesis 1:28
"And God blessed them [Adam and Eve], and God said unto them, 'Be fruitful and multiply, and replenish the earth'..."

Psalm 145:4
"One generation shall praise Thy works to another, and shall declare Thy mighty acts."

Joel 1:3
"Tell your children of it, and let your children tell their children, and their children another generation."

Psalm 78:2-7
"I will utter dark sayings of old: Which we have heard and known, and our fathers have told us. We will not hide them from their children, showing to the generation to come the praises of the LORD, and His strength, and His wonderful works that He hath done ... that they should make them known to their children: That the generation to come might know them, even the children which should be born; who should arise and declare them to their

children: That they might set their hope in God, and not forget the works of God, but keep His commandments."

It is God's plan to raise up godly families, who will raise up godly families, who will raise up godly families, and so on. Throughout history it can be seen that the strength of the nation depends on the strength of the church (Matt. 5:13), and the strength of the church depends on the strength of families (I Tim. 3:4-5). Many have this goal of raising up godly generations, but few people achieve it. If we want to achieve this goal in our life, we need to start now. But where do we start? We start with our present family; if we are children, that means our brothers and sisters. If present relationships are not strong, we are not laying a good foundation for the future. But if we can succeed now, we will have developed skills to succeed later.

Benefits of Being a Good Brother or Sister

- You will bring honor to your parents.
- You will have a good (powerful and effective) testimony to others.
- You will be laying a godly foundation for generations to come.
- You will get more accomplished (because you will have cooperation instead of conflicts).
- You will experience a peaceful home.
- You will be building vital character traits of godliness in your life.
- You will have excellent preparation for your future marriage and ministry.
- Your investment in the life of your sister or brother will be a priceless treasure to them.
- You and your siblings will avoid the trap of needing approval from friends, because you will find security in each other.
- Your love will be a demonstration to everyone that you are Christ's disciple. (John 13:35)
- Your brothers and sisters will be one of your greatest resources of caution, counsel, and help in times of need.
- You will find great joy!
- You will enjoy the rich, lifelong friendship that God intended.
- You will gain experience and insight which will help you get along with other believers—your brothers and sisters in Christ.

If you think that your brothers and sisters are so bad that you can never experience the things we've just mentioned, then you've missed the point. No matter how "bad" they are, you can still have these benefits if you are a good brother or sister to them.

When I was three years old, my mom and dad were told they could not have any more children. This came as a terrible blow, especially since they had intentionally postponed having children for a number of years before I was born. They were repentant. They now felt two weights of regret. One was that they would have no more children; the other was that I would not have brothers or sisters. Eventually, they decided to adopt. They did this with some fear and trembling, but they pursued it because they felt that the best gift they could give me was a brother or sister. They were right, but what if I missed the blessing by not having a good relationship with that brother or sister? Stephen was adopted when I was six and God miraculously gave us Grace three years later. They have truly been wonderful gifts. But what if I did not give them attention or care about them? What if we did not get along? What if I had considered them nuisances instead of God's blessings?

New perspectives often give new motivation. Ask the Lord to help you look at your relationship with your brothers and sisters from His perspective. Several years ago I was thinking about Stephen and Grace. I felt that we had a good relationship, but I began to wonder, "Is there anything I could do to strengthen our friendship and cause us to become even closer? I don't want to settle for average." Guess what? The Lord gave me an idea. It was only a little idea, but it worked better than I expected, and has brought us together in a special way. It's something anybody can do and, in fact, I've shared it with many friends, and quite a few of them have tried it. Many of them have given me a report of how well it has worked. I will explain all about this idea in chapter eleven. I strongly believe that if we do not have a close friendship with our brothers and sisters, we are missing out on one of the biggest blessings in life!

First Things First

The quality of our relationship with our brothers and sisters depends significantly upon our own relationship with the Lord. It is only by seeking His best in our *own* life first that we will then be able to have His best in our family. Because we are focusing on the bigger picture, we need to make each decision in light of eternity. This requires God's perspective. Here are three important foundations for you to check in your own life:

1. Cleanse Your Life

One essential step in seeking God's best is to get rid of any "polluting influence" that you are allowing in your life or home or family.

A Polluting Influence

Knock. Knock. No, this isn't a knock-knock joke. Someone was actually at our door. Stephen, Grace, and I answered the door and saw a very serious-looking neighbor with an urgent message. He warned my mom, "You might not want to let your kids go outside because there's a skunk in your backyard. It just went into your garage." We ran to the window and looked out. Sure enough, there it was. We were happy to see that the skunk walked out of our garage and across our backyard. Then we looked out our front window and saw a group of neighbors. Apparently, they had all seen the skunk a few minutes earlier and had been following this "polluting influence" as it had roamed through the neighborhood. (Our own "neighborhood watch" program at work.) Stephen, Grace, and I went out to join them. Since the skunk was out during the middle of the afternoon, they were worried that it might have rabies, and were discussing what to do.

More neighbors joined us, wondering what the exciting commotion in our neighborhood was all about. We all followed the skunk—from a distance. He crossed the street and walked to the end of the block. We noticed another open garage door and, apparently, so did the skunk. "Uh-oh," we thought, "the skunk is walking in that direction." Just as we feared, the skunk, who was looking for a place to hide, walked right in. Unfortunately, the family who lived there was not home. The neighbors were discussing the situation and still wondering what they should do. Then one courageous lady ran up to the garage and shut the garage door. "Hurray! We caught him! The neighborhood is safe!"

In the midst of this commotion, guess what happened? The family who lived there came home. They pulled into the driveway and saw a whole group of neighbors standing in their yard. They had not been expecting a welcoming committee. Before they had a chance to ask what was going on, the neighbor lady explained to them, "We have good news and bad news. The good news is we caught the skunk!" Then she couldn't help but grin. I don't know what they thought when they heard the bad news, "It's in ... um ... your garage."

BEING IN A POSITION OF LEADERSHIP IS A LONELY JOB

What polluting influences are in your life? How about things that are spiritually polluting?

- Corrupt Music (I Jn. 2:15)
- Bad Books (Acts 19:19)
- Tempting Magazines (I Jn. 2:16)
- Worldly TV shows (Ps. 119:37) (II Cor. 6:17)
- Unclean Videos (II Cor. 7:1)
- Occult Symbols (I Cor 10:22)
- Impure Pictures (Ps. 101:3)
- Wrong Words (Matt. 15:18)
- Evil Friends (Prov. 13:20)
- Toys or Objects with occult features, demonic names, double meanings, or representing ungodly things. (Ex. 20:4) (Dt. 7:26)

The End of the Skunk Story

What would you have done about the skunk in the garage? How were these neighbors going to get rid of it? They didn't want to let it out again. It might have rabies and be dangerous. What should they do? What would you do? Build a trap? Call the newspaper? Borrow a gun? Not open the garage door until he starves?

Instead of trying some unique or fancy idea, our neighbors decided to call in the experts. (No, not their dogs—the Humane Society.) Soon a pick-up truck pulled up and out stepped a man with a black bag. You'll never guess what he did. He walked right into the garage!! We watched from a distance as he went into the garage (with the black bag) ... and ... walked out of the garage (with the black bag) ... and drove off. He didn't smell. Don't ask us how he did that!

Our family has learned how important it is to keep our house and life clean from polluting influences. On various occasions, our family has made a group effort to cleanse our home. That means we go on a search to find any items which are inappropriate, have occult connections in any way, or could be a negative influence. We gather them together, have a family discussion, and dispose of them. (See Acts 19:17-19.)

2. Spend Time with the Lord and His Word

When I was eleven years old, I made the decision to begin having my own devotions every day. I had tried before and failed, but this time I was serious. I found a notebook to record what I learned and was excited to make God's Word a new priority in my life. This was one of the very best decisions I ever made. As I look back over my life now, I see that it was when I made this commitment at age eleven that I began to grow spiritually. It was about this time that I began to seek the Lord for myself, look for ways to please Him, and get to know Him more personally.

Our goal, as you remember, is to look at the future picture. It is being in God's Word that will give us this eternal perspective. None of us can expect to grow in our walk with the Lord unless we are seeing each step by the light that His Word sheds. If you have been neglecting your time with the Lord, do not let even one more day go by without establishing this as priority in your life.

The strings on Mom's violin bow had been eaten by a moth so she went to the store to buy mothballs. She didn't need them all for her violin case so she put some of them in my closet. Later that year our family took a trip and I needed a certain small bag for my packing. As I took this bag out of my closet, I began to cough. The bag smelled horrible because it had been right next to the mothballs in my closet. I washed my bag several times but was unable to get the smell out. Finally, I just packed it and we left on our trip. One day during our trip, I was standing in a big building talking with a young lady. Suddenly, she began looking around and said, "Boy, this building really smells like mothballs!" I tried not to laugh and decided not to stand too close to people.

My bag had been sitting next to mothballs all year, and therefore, gave off a mothball odor. In the same way, each of us will be either a "polluting influence" or a godly influence to those around us. God desires that we spread the fragrance of Christ everywhere we go. We want to saturate our community with the fragrance of Christ. Our godly attitudes, purity, and willingness to stand for Christ will spread His fragrance. Just as my bag spent its time sitting next to mothballs, so we want to spend our time with Jesus. If we are abiding in Christ and His Word, His fragrance will automatically flow from us. *"Now thanks be unto God, which always causeth us to triumph in Christ, and maketh manifest the savor [fragrance] of His knowledge by us in every place."* (II Cor. 2:14)

3. Submit to Your Parents

Would you like things to go well in your life? Do you want God's blessing? There is a third thing you should do.

One evening when I was twelve years old, I was confused, frustrated, and upset with Stephen. I was complaining about him to Mom and Dad and I didn't feel like being nice to him. Actually, I was sitting on my bed pouting. You might be guessing that Stephen and I had just had a big fight or argument, but that's not what happened. Actually, I can't remember why I was upset with Stephen, because, truthfully, Stephen was not the problem. I was upset with my dad and I was taking it out on Stephen. You see, I felt that Dad had done something better for Stephen than for me. I said it wasn't fair and that Dad liked Stephen better. If I had just been willing to resolve the problem with Dad, the whole thing would have been cleared up, and I would have started treating Stephen better. Many problems with brothers and sisters are confusing to us and difficult to work out, because underneath everything there are problems brewing with our parents, too. On the other hand, many problems would be solved if we would just submit to our parents and follow their advice.

Parental authority is a concept that most people do not seem to grasp. One of the main things that people have difficulty understanding about authority is that it is a **good** thing, not a **bad** thing. It is desirable—not undesirable. Here's why. God is the author of the world. He has all authority. But He has delegated authority to different people. God then works through these human authorities which He has set in place to accomplish His work in this world. (Rom. 13:1-5) If we are willing to be under our parents' authority, we will be protected from many wrong decisions and problems. Our parents will give us wisdom, caution, and direction. They must give account to God. This commandment is so important to God that He attached a special promise to it for those who honor it. Ephesians 6:2-3 tells us that this promise can apply to us today. It says, *"Honour thy father and mother; which is the first commandment with promise; That it may be well with thee, and thou mayest live long on the earth."* Few promises are better than that.

What if your parents are wrong and unreasonable? As long as what they ask you to do is not sin, obey them anyway, and let God work out the rest. Remember, you aren't really obeying them. You are obeying God and there is a promise attached. God's promises are true and exciting. We should take them seriously.

STEPHEN'S SECTION

Get Your Stuff Out of Here

It all started very simply. Our house is not very big so it is hard to find enough room for everything. Once when Sarah was about fourteen years old and I was about eight, Sarah was complaining that she didn't have enough room in her desk. The real problem is that she had too much stuff. Anyway, I had a desk with a lot of drawers, and since I don't save as much stuff as some other family members (names have not been listed to protect the author), some of the drawers were empty. Sarah asked me, "Since your drawers are empty, could I use some of them?" Can you believe it? She actually asked for one of MY drawers for HER stuff! I (being the shrewd businessman that I am) said, "Sure! But for a price." I made a deal with her. I rented it out for six months for a reasonable fee and we both signed the rental agreement.

About **ten** months later, I said, "Sarah, get your junk out of my drawer! Your time is up." She replied, "I don't have anywhere else to put it. I want to keep renting it." But I said, "No, I'm not making that deal again." She said, "You have to! I have nowhere else to put it." The pressure built, we began to state our views more strongly, neither of us could see any negotiable options, and the argument continued. Finally, I (being the shrewd businessmen that I am) took the drawer and dumped everything on the floor.

Sarah and I couldn't see things from the same perspective. I couldn't grasp that she had nowhere else to put her junk (why not the middle of her room?) and she didn't understand that six months means six months. When we get into an argument with our siblings, it would help if we could understand what they are thinking and how they feel. Probably we ourselves have been in the very same situation that they are in now. We need to step back and see how this is going to affect us in a year, two years, twenty years, or for eternity. Is having her stuff in my desk going to affect me in twenty years? Probably not. But if we have a bad relationship because we always argue, that will affect us the rest of our lives.

A friend of mine made a foolish decision because he was only looking at the small picture. Everyday when he came home from school, he would get off at a different bus stop than his sister so that he wouldn't have to walk home with her. I guess he was embarrassed by her and didn't want anyone to know that they were related. He was obviously more

concerned about what his friends thought than what the Lord thought. I doubt he ever considered how she felt. I wonder how his decisions would have changed if he could have seen how this would affect him in twenty years. He probably won't have those same friends, but he will still have the same sister, and the hurt that he caused her will last.

When my dad was growing up he had a dog named Browny and a cat named Whitey. (He named them. I didn't.) You're probably thinking that this is a story about a dog and cat who had major problems with each other. Not this time. Since my dad got Browny and Whitey at the same time, when they were just a puppy and kitten, they grew up together. They got along great. Browny would chase away other cats, but at night Browny and Whitey would curl up in the same box. The key factor is that they were close when they were little.

My dad said a similar situation is that of old friends. Often your best friends are old friends. You have bonds that were formed when you were young and now these people are special to you. You are close to them and relaxed with them. You trust each other and share many memories. All this is true, even though you may now have differences. The differences are ignored because you are old friends.

Well, who have you known the longest? Who knows you the best? It should be your brothers and sisters. They should be your best friends for life!

For many people this is not true! Why? It is because when they were young they simply tolerated their brothers and sisters but they weren't close. They weren't best friends. They allowed conflicts to exist and continue unresolved. They weren't thinking of the big picture—of eternity. They were only thinking of the "now." It's worth sacrificing the "now" for the future.

Stephen's Definitions

Perplexed — One boy who must write one sentence.

Confused — One boy who must write one paragraph.

Disaster — One boy who has a deadline set by his sister!

Skunk — A creature with enough "scents" not to play hide and seek.

Future — A time to schedule all of your work.

Yesterday — When your work was due.

Life — That thing that happens while you are busy doing something.

Campers — Nature's way of feeding mosquitoes.

GRACE'S SECTION

Seeing the Bigger Picture

- One time our family had two cars at a meeting and I wanted to ride home with Sarah and Stephen, but they told me I had to ride home with Mom and Dad. I didn't understand why Sarah and Stephen didn't want me to go with them, but that's because I couldn't see the big picture. Later, I found out that they were stopping to buy my Christmas present!
- One time when my sister, Sarah, was about six years old, she lost a friend because she wouldn't give her friend a dandelion. Both Sarah and the other girl were only looking at the tiny picture, weren't they? A dandelion isn't important, but it seemed to be important to them at the time.
- One time a sister and brother told Sarah that they hated each other and wished the other had not been born. What they didn't realize was that many struggles were ahead for their family and God had given them each other for a reason. They were going to need each other's support and help.
- One time a boy didn't give his little brother the attention and acceptance he needed. Later, he said that this was the biggest mistake he made in his life. But at the time he couldn't see the big picture. He didn't realize the influence he could have had as an older brother.
- One time eleven men thought their future was ruined because their leader was crucified on a cross. They didn't know that this was God's plan to save the whole world.

Being an Eagle and Not a Chicken

We want to see the bigger picture. I would rather be an eagle and be able to see everything from the air, than a chicken and just see my own little part of life. We need to see things from our sibling's perspective so that we can understand them. An eagle sees things from above. A chicken just sees little parts of the ground. We need to see things from God's perspective, and see how He uses everything in life to fit together for His purposes.

My Humming-Fly

A few years ago I was in Minnesota and met a man making balloon animals. As soon as I saw them, I thought they were neat, so I asked him if he would make me a butterfly. On our way home I was playing with my butterfly. I liked it a lot and named it "Honey!" (I always name my pet animals.)

I was having a lot of fun until all of a sudden—you guessed it ... POP! Oh, no! I picked it up and found that the two lower wings had popped. I was sad, but as I looked at it more closely, I saw that it now looked like a hummingbird! Then I remembered the Bible verse about how God works all things together for good for those who love Him. (Rom. 8:28) I actually liked my hummingbird (or "humming-fly!") even better than my butterfly! And I still kept it's name, "Honey!"

As Sarah, Stephen, and I are growing older, our relationship is changing. We used to play Legos and games together, but now we like to talk, laugh, and do projects together. We haven't drifted apart because of our own separate friends, interests, and schedules. No, our relationship stays strong. It is like the butterfly—it changes and the relationship then becomes a hummingbird. It is still nice, just different. And I am sure our relationship will change more and more as we get older. If we can learn to love and work well with our families as we're growing up, it will help us when we need to get along with other people in life.

Two Choices

Some brothers and sisters remain best friends all their lives. Others just see each other occasionally at family reunions and maybe send a Christmas card. Which do you want? The reason that many adults don't have a very close relationship with their brothers and sisters is because of offenses that happened when they were little and were never cleared up. We want the best. We want to be truly close. We aren't just trying to survive. Right now we shouldn't only think of the present, but we need to "look down the road," as my dad would say. We have a long life ahead and a lot of battles we have to fight together—but not against each other. We need to be on the same side.

Unexpected problems may await you when you don't look down the road. I am going to tell you about a time when my dad wasn't looking down the road.

Our whole family was in the car. My dad was driving. There was a bright, full moon. An owl had just awakened and found some breakfast.

Then he found a nice, flat, dry place to eat his meal—the highway. I guess it seemed comfortable and quiet at 1:00 A.M. While Mr. Owl was enjoying his breakfast, our family was enjoying a nice trip in the car. (At least, I hope we were ... I don't know for sure because I was sleeping.)

Little did that poor owl know the danger he was in, and little did our license plate know what was going to happen to it. Mr. Owl suddenly heard a noise behind him. He turned his head just in time to look right into, and I mean **right into**, a license plate. It was our car. My dad is a good driver but he came up over a hill and ... right in the middle of the road stood the owl. The license plate and the poor owl's nose had a slight collision.

Life is just like this story. My dad was driving the car but he couldn't see over the hill. Likewise, there will be times in our life when we can't see over the hill ahead of us. Brothers and sisters can prepare for the future by building a strong relationship now, so that later they will be able to hold each other accountable to do what is right, and help each other in the hard times that may await them over the hills of life.

TUBING THE RAPIDS
From Three Perspectives

Beginning Our Trip (August, 2001)

Sarah: It seemed to take longer than usual (and what's "usual" is usually a long time) for everyone to wake up, get dressed, finish morning devotions, eat breakfast, and pack things up at the campsite. Finally, we were on our way, anxious to rent tubes and travel down the river. On the way there, we tried to persuade Mom to go with us, but we were not too hopeful. The more we explained how fun, exciting, and adventurous it would be, the less interested Mom became.

We put on liberal amounts of sunscreen and headed toward the water. It took at least 45 minutes to rent the tubes due to the lack of decisiveness of certain members of the family, but at last we were ready to go. As we returned to the van to put on one last coat of sunscreen, we heard Mom timidly say, "I kind of wish I was going."

"You do?" we all said in shock, "Well, come then!" The three of us successfully convinced her by explaining that the leisurely route would be gentle and calm, and she wouldn't want to miss out on the fun. We headed toward the water again, but we hadn't made it very far when Dad said, "I forgot to put on sunscreen."

"You did?" we all said in disbelief, "What were you doing all that time?" Of course, we revisited the van for yet another coat of sunscreen. With excitement and anticipation, we hurried toward the water, but we were again stopped by Dad's voice. He said, "Did you put sunscreen on your ears?"

"No," we answered. After Dad's detailed explanation of why this was important, we made one more trip to the van. Convinced that four coats of sunscreen was definitely enough, we were ready to begin our adventure.

Stephen: Zion National Park is a great place to visit. My one suggestion is that you bring a lot of sunscreen. As we began our day on the river, I noticed that my bottle was empty. I had no idea that when I told Sarah she could use my sunscreen, I would get it back empty. I was the only one in the family that remembered to bring any. (Funny, since I'm the only one who doesn't need it.) It was the expensive kind, too, but anyway, that was not my only test in patience. You see, I thought we were going tubing right after breakfast. I don't mind waiting a reasonable amount of time. (I understand that some people are not as talented in punctuality as I am.) But in my opinion, 2:00 in the afternoon is *not* right after breakfast.

Grace: It was a wonderful start to a wonderful day. After a nice morning at the campsite and getting well prepared for the day, we left for the river. Stephen and Sarah did complicate things a little by rushing around so much. After all, vacations are when you're supposed to relax, not rush, right? Even so, I didn't let them bother me, and we had a nice start to the day.

On the River

Sarah: After our strenuous morning, we were finally in the water. The sunlight was shining through the trees, the water was warm, and the scenery was lovely. We were all floating down the river in our little rubber rafts. The best part was the rapids. No, actually, the best part was watching my parents; it was quite entertaining. They were having a harder time than the three of us, who were floating leisurely down the river. Grace was cute, as she drifted with ease and looked at the sky. "This is the life!" she said with satisfaction.

I was enjoying the ride when all of a sudden, "Ouch!" My hair caught a branch and flipped me underwater. My tube kept going but I did not. I was stuck by my hair. Fortunately, I have a little brother who is very sensitive to my needs. In a flash, he came to my rescue. He helped me untangle my hair and soon I was free. I was slightly alarmed when I heard him mention the word, "knife," but fortunately, he didn't have it with him.

Stephen: Well, when you are tubing you can only see a little ahead of you—up to the next bend. There were rapids, jagged rocks, sand, mud, deep water, logs, branches, trees, and sharp turns, so you would always have to be trying to turn and steer yourself around these. It also began to rain and I was worried about those dark clouds moving in. I didn't have time to worry too much, though, because I was trying to keep track of everyone else.

Mom had the most trouble. She was always last. She just couldn't seem to get around the rocks, through narrow places, or back into the current (or get into the current in the first place). Besides that, she always seemed to manage to go down all of the rapids backwards. Mom never knew where she was going, and was always out of control. We kept hearing her say, "Oh, no! Oh, no!"

Dad was taking the whole ride very seriously. He liked to kneel on all fours up on top of his tube. He said that this gave him more mobility, balance, and protection. (Whatever!) In a serious tone of voice he would call out directions to everyone else.

Grace was leisurely floating down the river, watching my parents who were behind us. "Watch out! Here come some big rapids!" we heard Dad call to Mom who, as usual, was going backwards. Grace was looking back at my parents and laughing. In fact, she was so interested in watching them that she forgot to watch where she was going. And then it happened. CRASH! She hit a tree trunk.

You already know about my emergency rescue for Sarah. As I was untangling her hair I said, "If only I had my knife," (which I usually carry with me, but I wasn't expecting to whittle any marshmallow sticks in the middle of the river). Sarah was shocked (I guess I should say more shocked, since she was already shocked from getting her hair stuck). She said, "A knife? For my hair?" Now who would ever think of a ridiculous question like that?

"No, silly, for the branch."

Grace: We had a great trip! It's a good thing Stephen was along. I didn't even notice when Sarah lost her tube and was caught by a tree branch. He notices everything. I noticed the sky! The clouds were beautiful!

Poor Mommy! She looked exhausted! I tried to tell her that you don't have to do anything but look at the sky and let your tube go. I tried

to explain to Daddy that he didn't need to be worried. I told him that no one was going to get hurt.

Stephen and Sarah thought it was funny when I hit a tree, but I don't care about what they think, do I? As I said before, the sky was worth looking at.

The Bigger Picture

Sarah: After our trip, our family had a talk about how life is similar to tubing down a river. You may have difficulties and surprises, but you keep pressing ahead anyway. You don't just merrily row your boat down the stream. (Life is **not** a dream.)

Stephen: Not only that, but when you're tubing you must remember that you cannot see the whole picture. You can only see up to the next bend and you don't know what is ahead. From the sky you can see the whole river and where you are going, but from down below you can only see the next step. We need to look at our life from God's perspective. Sometimes we only know the next task or the next step, but the Lord has a much bigger plan in store for us.

Grace: The point of having all three of us tell this story is to show you that each one of us has a different perspective. An important tool for getting along and working as a team is to understand things from another's viewpoint. And most importantly, we need to see things from God's bigger perspective. We need to relax and look up.

I'M PERPLEXED...

Question: What if the big picture looks dark and hopeless and I feel like giving up?

Answer: Then you feel like Elijah did when he was in the wilderness being chased by Queen Jezebel and was so discouraged that he asked to die (I Kgs. 19). You feel like Abraham who had great dreams for his family but had no children (Gen. 17). You feel like David when his own son revolted against him and tried to take the kingdom (II Sam. 15).

Looking back on each of these stories, we can now see that God had a bigger plan. These people were just not able to see it. To them things seemed hopeless and beyond repair—but the Lord had an amazing plan ready to unfold.

Many times the Lord does not show us the whole picture. He only shows us the next step. Faith is obeying even when we do not understand. Maybe things seem impossible in your family. Humanly, they are impossible. Maybe you cannot imagine any way that the Lord could work. This is simply an opportunity for the Lord to show Himself strong. Your job is to take the first step and do your best for Him right now. I Cor. 2:9 says, *"Eye hath not seen, nor ear heard, neither have entered into the heart of man, the things which God hath prepared for them that love Him."*

HIS Story Applied Today

Are You Sure Your Eyes Are Open?

Once there was a prophet in Israel who was annoying to the king of Syria because he kept exposing the Syrian's military plans. You see, secret intelligence has been important throughout history—not just today. Countries have used spies since the beginning of time. On this particular occasion, the king of Syria couldn't figure out how Israel always knew their plans and avoided their terrorism. Finally, he called a National Security Council meeting of his top military strategists and said, "We've got a leak. Someone among us is a spy."

But his advisors then explained to him, "That's not the case. A prophet in Israel, named Elisha, is able to tell the king of Israel the exact words you speak, even in your bedroom." And that was true. It had become common knowledge. Israel didn't try to hide this secret weapon. God told Elisha exactly what was being decided by Syria's military strategists in their Defense Department offices. You can't have better intelligence than that.

So Syria sent an army after Elisha. They had spies, too. They knew that Elisha was in Dothan, a medium-sized city in northern Israel. In the middle of the night they surrounded the city with horses and chariots and a large host of military combat units. At sunrise Elisha's servant looked out and saw their predicament. He was very fearful. He knew that they were the enemy's target. He asked Elisha, "What are we going to do?" He had seen God do many miracles through Elisha, but this was a whole army! How would they get out of this one? His faith was weak. He was young. Fear took over. He couldn't see the bigger picture.

Elisha said, "Fear not, for there are more with us than with them." Then Elisha prayed that God would open the young man's eyes. God did. Suddenly, he saw the whole mountain around the enemy filled with fiery horses and chariots. This was an angelic army of protection. Israel had more secret weapons than they realized. To learn the rest of the details, read II Kings 6.

Elisha's servant was scared to death because he was only looking at things from his own viewpoint. Once he could see things from God's perspective, everything totally changed. In the same way, we should pray that the Lord would open our eyes and allow us to see life from His perspective. Every decision, argument, action, and attitude will be changed when we see things from God's bigger picture.

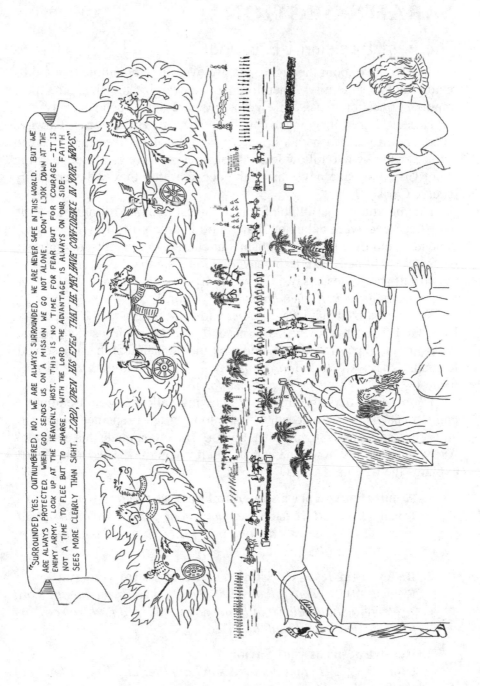

"Surrounded, yes. Outnumbered, no. We are always surrounded. We are never safe in this world. But we are always protected. When God sends us on a mission we go not alone. Don't look down at the enemy army. Look up at the heavenly host. This is no time for fear but for courage—it is not a time to flee but to charge. With the Lord the advantage is always on our side. Faith sees more clearly than sight. Lord, open his eyes that he may have confidence in your ways."

SARAH'S SECTION

The Best Decision I Ever Made

As we think about the bigger picture, we must remember that God's picture includes eternity. Therefore, as we examine our lives, the most important question to ask ourselves is, "Where will I spend eternity?"

Because I grew up going to church and hearing Bible stories, I always considered myself to be a Christian. One day I realized that I had to choose on my own to follow Jesus. Many people have grown up learning about God, but have never made the decision that they will personally receive Christ.

Do you know what I think Satan's biggest lie is? Millions of people have been deceived, believing that "good people go to heaven." If we depend on our own life, our baptism, our church, our parents, or our good works, we will not make it to heaven. God's standard is perfection and we all fall short. Jesus says, *"I am the way, the truth, and the life: no man cometh unto the Father, but by Me."* (John 14:6)

When I realized that I was a sinner and that I deserved to be separated from God forever, I knew that I needed a rescuer. Jesus died on the cross for me to pay for my sin. He took the punishment that I deserved. Romans 5:8 says, *"But God commendeth His love toward us, in that, while we were yet sinners, Christ died for us."*

I came to understand that just "knowing" all this wasn't enough; I had to make a choice to accept Christ into my life. I repented of my sin, and accepted Jesus as my personal Savior. Have you made this decision? Are you sure that you will be in heaven after you die? The Bible clearly explains the way to heaven:

1. **Admit that you are a sinner and deserve to go to hell.**
   Isaiah 53:6 *"All we like sheep have gone astray; we have turned every one to his own way; and the LORD hath laid on Him the iniquity of us all."*

2. **Believe that Jesus Christ died on the cross for your sin.**
   Romans 10:9 *"That if thou shalt confess with thy mouth the Lord Jesus, and shalt believe in thine heart that God hath raised Him from the dead, thou shalt be saved."*

3. **Receive Jesus as your Savior.**
   I John 5:12 *"He that hath the Son hath life; and he that hath not the Son of God hath not life."*

How Well Do You Know About Brothers and Sisters in the Bible?

Match the correct person with the correct situation:

A. Cain
B. The prodigal son
C. Mary
D. Peter
E. Eliab
F. Joseph

G. Martha
H. David
I. Miriam
J. Brother of Prodigal Son
K. Jacob
L. Leah

1. __F__ I can honestly tell you that God used the horrible and dreadful actions of my brothers for good—yes, for good! Who am I?

2. __L__ I lived in continuous tension because of the competition between my sister and me. Who am I?

3. __C__ The many expectations of my older sister caused difficulties for me. Who am I?

4. __H__ My older brother falsely accused me, but all I wanted to do was to fight the battles of the Lord. Who am I?

5. __A__ I was severely punished by God because of the way I treated my younger brother. Who am I?

6. __B__ I looked to friends for security and happiness, instead of to my family. In the end, I found out that my family were much better friends than all those others I'd been trying to please. Who am I?

7. __K__ I was forced to run away from home because I made my brother so angry with me. Who am I?

8. __I__ The course of history was affected because I made a wise decision when I was babysitting my brother. Who am I?

9. __E__ My younger brother was demonstrating the courage and initiative I knew I should have had. But instead of confessing any guilt, I just blamed my brother. Who am I?

10. __D__ I was willing to listen to my brother and was therefore, introduced to a very important individual. Who am I?

11. __J__ Many family conflicts resulted because I did not show compassion or forgiveness to my younger brother. My father was especially hurt by this. Who am I?

12. __G__ I was frustrated and irritated because my sister did not have the same priorities as I did. Who am I?

For answers to quiz see next page.

Answers to: How Well Do You Know About Brothers and Sisters in the Bible?

1. Joseph
2. Leah
3. Mary
4. David
5. Cain
6. The prodigal son
7. Jacob
8. Miriam
9. Eliab
10. Peter
11. Brother of the prodigal son
12. Martha

CHAPTER FOUR

Problems Come and Problems Stay!

Finding the Root Problem

STEPHEN'S SECTION

The Unwanted Stranger
August, 1999

This is Reporter Mailbox for Mally News Eyewitness, and I'm here with a unique situation to bring to your attention. Let me describe to you the picture here on the scene. It's late at night at Grandma Mally's house. Strangely enough, Dad, Grace, and Stephen are sitting in the car holding flashlights and baseball bats. Let me assure you, this is not their normal practice. Something strange must be up. Let's find out what is going on...

"Excuse me, Grace, I'm Reporter Mailbox with Mally News Eyewitness. May I ask you a few questions?"

"Sure, go ahead."

"What on earth are you doing—sitting in a car late at night? Flashlights? Baseball bats?"

"Well, Mailbox, the story began last winter. Dad needed to do some work under the house. He was crawling on his stomach, in the crawl space underneath the house, when all of a sudden he saw two eyes looking at him. He heard a growl and found himself face to face with a possum (a big one!). Needless to say, Dad decided his project could wait."

"I see, Grace, so what are you doing now?"

"We don't like this unwanted stranger living under Grandma's house, so we've got a plan to get rid of him. We're waiting for the possum to come out (they come out at night). When he does, we're going to shine our flashlights at him. We've heard that if a possum looks straight at the light, he won't be able to see anything else and he won't move. While Dad and I are holding the flashlights, Stephen is going to creep around behind him and clobber him over the head with a baseball bat." (Apologies to animal lovers everywhere.)

"Thank you, Grace. You have been very helpful." Well, there you have it, folks—trying to kill a possum with a baseball bat. For Mally News Eyewitness, I'm Reporter Mailbox.

Several Weeks Later...

Hello, Reporter Mailbox here, with Mally News Eyewitness, back to bring you an up-to-date report on the unwanted stranger. I'm sorry to say the late night clobber endeavor was unsuccessful. The possum never

came out. After waiting and waiting, the three troopers got tired, hungry, and bored, and they gave up.

Right now, I'm again standing in Grandma Mally's yard (that's where I spend most of my time) and as much as I can tell, Dad, Stephen, and Grace are running around the house in the dark. They're playing night time hide and seek.

Wait, I hear a yell. It sounds like Grace is alone in the back yard. "Help! Dad, Stephen, quick! I see the possum!" (I guess they weren't the only ones playing hide and seek.) "There he is!"

The chase is on. There goes the possum. There go Grace, Dad, and Stephen close behind him. Uh-oh, he ran under the oil tank. Now what? It seems that Dad has a plan. He's telling Grace to go inside and get Sarah, Mom, and the baseball bats. Not this again!

Here they come, but Sarah and Mom don't look too excited. "Come on you guys; get in the spirit! It's not that often you get to go possum hunting!"

There he is! We can see him hiding in the pile of stuff (junk) behind the shed. Dad is blocking one exit. Sarah, Grace, and Mom are blocking another exit and banging around and making a lot of noise to scare him out. There is only one other possible exit, and Stephen is standing by that exit with the baseball bat raised and ready to ... well, you know what. (Apologies to animal lovers everywhere.)

Now it's 11:30 P.M., and the people next door are probably wondering what their crazy neighbors are doing running around with flashlights and baseball bats and making such a racket.

But back to the story. What? Sarah, Mom, and Grace are going inside to bed? What's wrong with them? We were just getting to the exciting part!

"Hello, Mr. Mally, I'm Reporter Mailbox with Mally News Eyewitness. The possum won't come out and your troops went in. Things aren't going too well, are they? What's your plan now?"

"Let's block the exits so he's trapped under the oil tank. Then we'll block the entrance to his home so that if he escapes from the trap, at least he can't keep living under Grandma's house. And one more thing—let's go to bed."

Two Years Later...

This is Reporter Mailbox to bring you the conclusion of the story. The good news is that the possum left. The bad news is that he came back. He's still living under the house, much to the Mally's grief. (So I guess it's not a conclusion at all, but it's a happy ending for all you animal lovers.) Until next time, I'm Reporter Mailbox with Mally News Eyewitness.

What's Underneath Your House?

You may be wondering why I told the story of our adventure with the possum. You're probably thinking, "I'm trying to get along with my siblings, not with possums." Well, one of the reasons some siblings can't get along is because there are unresolved problems between them. These problems may not be visible to everybody, but you know that they are still living underneath your house.

From the possum story we learned that our problems won't go away by themselves. It's not good enough merely to make sure he stays under the house out of sight. It won't work to just forget about him. He'll show up someday when you are not expecting him. Nor can you simply chase him away because he will come back. We learned that the hard way! This "unwanted stranger" is not something you can get rid of with baseball bats or traps. It's harder than that. But if you let him stay, he will be a constant hindrance and obstacle. The first step to improve relationships is to get rid of the "unwanted stranger."

As much as I hate to do this, I had better tell you a personal example. When Grace and I make our beds we have a race to see who can get done first. Usually, I win. One particular day, a particular person wasn't too happy because I got a head start. Grace decided that her only chance to win would be to slow me down. Her strategy was to yank the comforter off of my bed and attempt to wrap it around my head. Well, that was a mistake; I was already having a bad day. So I became upset and decided to tie her up in our all-purpose comforter. Somehow, something happened to someone at sometime, somewhere by someone ... or something like that. (Don't ask for any specifics.) Anyway, Grace got hurt and left the room crying. Now, I could just try to forget about it, but that would be like leaving the possum under the house. I could just try to be nice to her, but the "unwanted stranger" would still be there. So what should I do? You'll find out in the next chapter.

Stephen's Definitions

Flashlight — A container for dead batteries.

Forgiveness — Not in most people's vocabulary.

My philosophy — Do it tomorrow. I've already made enough mistakes for today.

Conscience — It doesn't keep you from doing anything, it just keeps you from enjoying it.

Temper — Wise people lose this permanently.

Sunscreen — Something that sisters only remember to wear on cloudy days.

Experience — The name we give our mistakes.

SARAH'S SECTION

Finding the Root Problems in Relationships

Our goal in this chapter is to help you identify and get rid of any "unwanted strangers" in your life. As you consider any problems in your relationship with your brothers or sisters, search for the "unwanted stranger." In other words, look for the underlying problem. Get below the symptoms that are on the surface and find the real cause.

These root problems are not only like possums, they are also like weeds. They start small (just a seed). You don't even think it's there at all (it disappears under the ground). But then one day the problem shows up (it has broken the surface of the ground). Now it will get worse and worse (weeds get big fast!). Therefore, we can't just deal with the surface issues of our problem (that would be like only breaking off the top of the weed). One must get rid of the problem itself—the root. True conquerors defeat the giant; they are not content to simply escape from him.

How do you find the root problem? Well, think of a recent conflict in your family, and then read the following story. Maybe this example from our family will help you do some evaluating. This happened quite a while ago (I was sixteen and Stephen was ten) but it is a good example of root problems.

All five of us were tired as we traveled home from a long trip. The car was worse than disorganized, and we were all anxious to get home. I was feeling miserable because I was coming down with a fever and cold. It was not a particularly good day. Can you relate? Even so, I think the day would have been fine if we had been getting along. Unfortunately, we were **not** getting along. Stephen and Grace were bickering, arguing, and annoying the rest of us. Actually, the main problem seemed to be Stephen. He was upset, complaining about everything, and would not cooperate with any of us ...

As you can see, there was a problem in our family. This was not the way it was supposed to be, but what was wrong? First, let's list the surface problems. Those are easy to find. In my story we see arguing, complaining, bad attitudes, and a lack of cooperation. You probably have different surface problems in your story. Some others might be disrespect, lying, bragging, silence, teasing, temper tantrums, or unkind words and actions. We can try to deal with these visible problems, but we will not be very successful unless we tackle the invisible problems first.

But invisible problems are difficult to find. On this last day of our trip, none of us knew why Stephen was acting this way. We were confused. His attitude was not typical. Something must be wrong, but what?...

Let me prepare you for the rest of the story. As you look for underground root problems, remember that a key thing to search for is bitterness. Here's why. When someone has been hurt or offended, they naturally respond by becoming angry. (This is a wrong response, of course, but we'll come back to this.) This anger builds and they become bitter at the one who hurt them. If the offense is not cleared up, the hurt and attitude of revenge does not go away. Even if they forget about the original problem, or fight, or whatever it was, a pattern of anger and bitterness has started. They, themselves, might not even realize this. All they know is that they easily get upset and irritated with this person. Certain topics or circumstances may cause flare-ups. The other person, also, is likely confused. "Why do they get so angry with me about such a small thing?" But you see, it's not really the small thing causing the anger—it's the offense behind it, of which this small thing reminds them. It was not dealt with the first time and so it easily comes back. This bitterness is an "unwanted stranger" that must not be allowed to stay.

"Follow peace with all men, and holiness, without which no man shall see the Lord: Looking diligently lest any man fail of the grace of God: **lest any root of bitterness springing up trouble you***, and thereby many be defiled."* (Heb. 12:14-15)

"Let all bitterness, and wrath, and anger, and clamor, and evil speaking be put away from you, with all malice." (Eph. 4:31)

... As our family was wondering why Stephen was having such a bad day, my parents were pondering what to do. They knew that his actions were only surface problems, but they had no idea what the root might be. Mom and Dad asked Stephen to come to the front seat of the van, so they could talk with him. Dad began to think about things that had happened earlier in the day. He remembered that Stephen and Grace had been in an argument that morning. Dad explained to Stephen, "I really don't know what's wrong, and you won't tell me. Maybe the problem has something to do with the argument that you had with Grace earlier. I don't know whose fault that was, but I know that you were the one blamed. Maybe we were wrong, and you received blame that you didn't deserve..."

Injustice is hard for anyone to handle. What is injustice? It is when someone is falsely criticized or accused or punished and they don't deserve it. A person automatically knows when he is treated unjustly, and most people are not able to respond properly. Instead, the deep pain produces a "get back at you" attitude. (That's bitterness and revenge.) It comes out in the surface problems we already mentioned, like pouting, criticizing, and arguing.

... Dad knew that injustice is often the key to problems, and that is what made him remember how Stephen had been blamed for the argument. My parents didn't say anything else to Stephen. All they had to do was acknowledge this possible injustice and Stephen's attitude totally changed. It was obvious that this had been the problem. Stephen had been unjustly accused and was reacting in all kinds of strange ways. Once this root cause was cleared up, Stephen completely changed. When we arrived home, he gladly helped to clean out the whole van. He was extremely cooperative and helpful, and he did more work than anyone else. As you can see, the way to clear up conflicts is to start with the root!

House Painting

Have you ever wished that you didn't have to scrape before you paint? I can still remember standing in the hot sun with Stephen, scraping and scraping. It seemed to take all summer just to scrape our house. I think that painting is more fun than scraping, don't you agree? But the scraping has to be done first. It is the same way with relationships. It is necessary that you apply chapters four and five before expecting success from other steps or ideas given in this book. You cannot simply move ahead without clearing up the past. If there are past offenses which you have never made right, you will not be able to have the right relationship with your sibling now, no matter how hard you try. You might have to dig deep. The root problem may not have happened this morning. There may be conflicts that happened five years ago which still have not been uncovered and resolved.

Perhaps we can learn some insights from the life of two brothers who had difficulties in their relationship, due to unresolved problems. The younger of the two was deceitful and tricked his older brother. One particular day, something happened which made the whole situation worse. He stole a certain item which was very valuable to his older brother. The older brother was deeply hurt and offended. The younger brother did not repent of the theft, or try to make it right, and his older brother became very bitter against him. It was impossible now for these two brothers to have a good relationship until this offense was made right. The older brother struggled with a growing anger and hatred toward his younger brother. Soon the younger brother lived in a constant fear of the older one. This situation only became worse, and finally, the older brother decided to kill his younger brother. The younger one was forced to run away from home. Their family was now separated and in turmoil. (Read Genesis 27 to learn more about Jacob and Esau.)

Many times we can deeply hurt and wound the spirit of our brother or sister without realizing what we are doing. As a result, there are "unwanted strangers," and we don't even know they exist.

Examine yourself for any ways you may have caused bitterness in your brother or sister. Learn to look at situations from their perspective. Ask yourself:

- Have I hurt them through unkind words or actions?
- Have I lied to them or stolen from them?
- Have I made fun of them or teased them? Especially in front of my friends? Or their friends?
- Have I neglected to do something that they were expecting from me?
- Have I been hard to please?
- Have I been angry with them or lost my temper?
- Have I been insensitive to their feelings?
- Have I treated them unjustly in any way?
- Have I put my own friends and priorities ahead of them?
- Have I gossiped against them?
- Have I caused frustration by not noticing or praising them?
- Have I had a competitive spirit against them?
- Have I failed to fulfill something I said I would do?
- Have I ignored them with an attitude of unconcern?

They Know Not What They Do

Now let's consider how **we** should respond when our siblings hurt **us**. Since our brothers and sisters are not perfect, they have probably wronged us in some way. Though it is difficult, it is our responsibility to respond correctly. We know that the wrong response is to become angry and bitter, but what is the right response? In chapters seven and eight, we will explain in more detail how to have correct responses to problems, but the main concept to understand in this chapter is the concept of forgiveness. Forgiving someone who has hurt us is one of the hardest things to do. Many times we think we have forgiven someone, but we are still upset with them, and hope that they get "paid back" for what they did. This is not forgiveness. True forgiveness is releasing them from any obligation

to us and holding nothing against them. If we have truly forgiven them, then we want the best for them, and we are happy when they succeed.

Three Keys to Forgiveness

- In order to forgive others, we should first remember how much we have been forgiven by God.
- Remember that people are like little lambs. Many do not have the teaching and leading of a good shepherd. That is why, when Jesus was suffering on the cross, He said about those who had mocked, ridiculed, and tortured Him unjustly, *"Father, forgive them; for they know not what they do."* (Luke 23:34)
- A third key to forgiveness is to ask why God let this injustice happen. There are several possible reasons:

  1. It is a test from God.
     He wants to reward us for successfully responding in a godly way.
  2. It is a temptation from Satan.
     He wants to produce ungodly responses, and thus destroy us through failure.
  3. It is an assignment.
     This is God's way of showing us this person's need. Maybe God wants us to pray for them, comfort them, show them compassion, do something good for them, or teach them.
  4. It is a source of unseen benefits which God wants to give us in an unusual way. If you can see these benefits, it will take away your anger, and you will immediately be able to thank God, take responsible action, and forgive.

Matthew 6:14-15 says, *"For if ye forgive men their trespasses, your Heavenly Father will also forgive you: But if ye forgive not men their trespasses, neither will your Father forgive your trespasses."*

GRACE'S SECTION

Root Problems

Root problems are when your flowers are sick. Charlie was a very sick tulip. He kept drooping over and couldn't stand up. He felt miserable and his leaves and petals were even beginning to turn brown. All the flowers were trying to figure out what was wrong with poor Charlie.

"Maybe something is wrong with his leaves," a daisy suggested. "They are so big and clumsy!"

Charlius Tulipus

A peony said, "I bet it is his petals ... They look a bit small."

"I don't think he has the right color," broke in a sweet pea. "I think he should be purple or pink."

"Well, flowers, I really think it must be his yellow middle. Maybe it doesn't have enough pollen," said the old sunflower, "or maybe the bees have been gathering too much nectar?"

"His stem doesn't look too healthy," commented the daffodil. "It keeps drooping and wobbling in the wind."

A few violets stated, "We think it is the thorn bush right beside him that is bothering him!"

"Maybe he is not planted in the right place," said the morning glory.

"Yes, that's it!" a few other flowers agreed.

But then along came the wisest of the flowers, the rose, and said, "Flowers! Flowers! Listen! The problem is his roots! Nothing is wrong with his petals, or his leaves, or his color. He is sick because his roots are sick!"

As it turned out, the rose was right; the problem was way down beneath the ground where no one could see. His roots were sick! Charlie's root problem was that he didn't have water!

Human Flowers

There is a human flower named Jenny. Jenny is ten years old and she can't get along with her two brothers. She just never feels like being nice to them. It all started when they took something of hers a long time ago. They broke it and that made Jenny really mad. This caused her to begin a pattern of anger towards them, and she always wanted to "get back." Her root problem is called bitterness.

And then, there is Johnny, for an example. He's a human flower, too, but some call him a weed. Actually, some even call him a thistle!

He causes a lot of trouble. He doesn't like anything his older sister does. The real problem is that he's jealous because he thinks his parents praise his older sister and not him. This makes Johnny always try to be better than his sister. I guess you could describe him like this: jealousy is his petals and scent. Fear and guilt are his two leaves. Pride is his stem. But revenge is his root, because he feels that his sister stole his parents from him.

I suppose I'm a human flower named Grace ...

One day our family was visiting my grandma in Illinois.

We were packing the car and about to leave for home. A few people in our family were discussing how two of our family members are so slow. This is questionable. Sometimes we are a little slower than the rest of the family, but that's because we think harder. We can be fast if we want to!

To continue my story, the certain three people were talking, laughing, and making jokes about how slow we are at gas stations. I became angry. In fact, I was so upset, I went and hid behind a bush in the backyard.

Why was I so upset? Why couldn't I just laugh with them? Why did I hide? What was the root problem? The first underlying problem was that I was thinking wrong thoughts about my family. I was believing lies! Lies like, "They don't care about me," "They must like to hurt me," "I have the right to be angry—they were so mean to me!" "They only think about themselves—they don't even care if I am sad," and "They are so insensitive!"

If you had seen me there behind the bush, you would have seen only the surface problems. I was crying, grumpy, and wouldn't talk to anyone. You could have tried to talk to me about these things, but it wouldn't have helped, because that wasn't the real problem. The real problem was that I allowed myself to believe lies about my family. I became more and more angry over just a little joke and I wanted to get back at them. This is why I hid. I wanted them to get worried and come looking for me. I knew they wanted to leave right away, so by hiding, I could get back at them.

To conclude the story, my dad came and found me behind the bush and brought me back to the van. I wouldn't talk to anyone for awhile. But when my family knew how upset I was, they felt bad. My mom always comforts me when I am sad. The whole family felt sorry about what happened.

My parents helped me, later, to understand what happened. First, I had felt that I was receiving treatment that I didn't deserve. Then I responded wrongly by allowing myself to believe untrue thoughts. This produced a bitter attitude in me.

Root problems are important to flowers (whether they are real flowers or human). Even though problems at the root are invisible, they make everything else sick. But like Charlie, Jenny, Johnny, and Grace, once you know what is wrong with the root, you know what to do to fix the problem.

HIS STORY APPLIED TODAY

From Jealousy to Hatred

If you fight with your brother, you are not the only one. The very first brothers on earth had a big fight. Their names were Cain and Abel. They had no bad TV shows, bad friends, bad books, or wrong music to influence them, but they still had problems. Big problems!

Cain and Abel both brought an offering to the Lord. I expect they both put much care and work into their sacrifice. There was one major difference. Cain brought the wrong offering and Abel brought the right one. The Lord was pleased with Abel's sacrifice, but not with Cain's. Cain was very angry and downcast. The Lord explained to Cain that if he did right he would be accepted, but God also warned him that sin was right outside the door.

Cain was angry that Abel was accepted and he was not. To obey God would mean humbling himself before his younger brother. His pride would not let him do that. He was not about to admit that his little brother was right and he was wrong. That would be too humiliating. Instead of seeking to do what was right, he condemned Abel's righteous standards. Cain's root problem of bitterness was not dealt with. His jealousy and anger built up and the only solution he could think of was to get rid of Abel.

"For this is the message that ye heard from the beginning, that we should love one another. Not as Cain, who was of that wicked one, and slew his brother. And wherefore slew he him? Because his own works were evil, and his brother's righteous." (I Jn. 3:11-12)

"DO YOU REALLY THINK YOU SHOULD TAKE HERBS FROM THE FIELD? I WONDER IF THE LORD WILL BE PLEASED. HE HAS ALWAYS DESIRED A LAMB. DON'T YOU REMEMBER HOW FATHER EXPLAINED DEATH TO US?"

"JUST BE QUIET. YOU THINK YOU'RE ALWAYS RIGHT. I DO WHAT I WANT TO DO. YOU DON'T KNOW EVERYTHING."

I'M PERPLEXED...

Question: How do I know if I'm bitter?

Answer: None of us ever want to admit that we might be bitter. It sounds like too strong of a word. "Surely, it's not that bad," we think. Remember, though, that bitterness starts small and builds. If we are overly irritated by small things someone does, if we see everything they do as wrong, if we have internal anger or feelings of hatred toward them, or if we are unable to forgive them, these are signs of bitterness.

Question: Is bitterness always the root problem?

Answer: No, but when it comes to relationships, bitterness is a main one. I John 2:16 says, *"For all that is in the world, the lust of the flesh, and the lust of the eyes, and the pride of life, is not of the Father, but is of the world."* These sins (immorality, greed, and pride) seem to be the root causes behind most other sins. Bitterness can often be traced back to pride, and pride is the main obstacle to correcting every case of bitterness.

Self-Evaluation Quiz 4

1. **My brother/sister and I are...**
   ☒ Close.
   ☒ Loyal friends.
   ❑ Repelling magnets.
   ☒ Related.
   ❑ Unpredictable.

2. **My relationship with my brother/sister would best be compared to...**
   ☒ A football game.
   ❑ A tornado.
   ❑ World War II.
   ☒ A jigsaw puzzle which fits together perfectly, if you work on it long enough.

3. **Having a life-long relationship with my siblings is...**
   ☒ My goal.
   ❑ A brand new idea.
   ❑ An oxymoron.
   ❑ A nice, but seemingly impossible idea.
   ☒ Something that has already begun in our lives

4. **When I begin to search for the root problem...**
   ❑ I keep thinking that my brother is the "unwanted stranger."
   ☒ I realize why I react the way I do.
   ☒ I find that the Bible is the best magnifying glass.

5. **My brother/sister knows that he/she is more important to me than any friend.**
   ❑ Yes, of course.
   ☒ I hope so.
   ❑ I've never thought of that before.
   ❑ You would have to ask them. How would I know?

6. **When my mom blames me for something my sister did, my usual response is...**
   ☒ Blame my little sister, of course.
   ❑ Play dead.
   ❑ Collect fingerprints, gather witnesses, compile legal documents, and call my lawyer.
   ❑ Begin to explain the situation with a humble attitude.

CHAPTER FIVE

Peace Treaties in the Living Room

Healing Hurt Relationships

SARAH'S SECTION

Healing Hurt Relationships

"We read chapter four!" you say. "We found the unwanted stranger! Now how do we get rid of him? How do we clear up these root problems?"

Let me begin by warning you that this will not be easy. In fact, this may be the hardest chapter of the book to apply. If you can make it through this one, you are on your way to victory.

One Saturday morning, a number of years ago, I was sitting on my bed reading. My parents had gone out for breakfast and Stephen and Grace were downstairs playing. The silence was broken by a loud scream, "SARAH, SARAH! COME HERE! **QUICK!**" Stephen and Grace were yelling for me to come downstairs. This is certainly not the normal way they call for me, so I knew immediately that something was wrong. I jumped out of bed and raced downstairs. There I found both Stephen and Grace in tears.

Stephen said, "Grace has a nail stuck in her foot and we can't get it out." I looked and saw a very scared Grace with a large nail sticking out of her foot. I figured that the first thing to do would be to get the nail out. Taking a deep breath, I sat her down, gently took her foot, and pulled the nail. As I did this, she jerked and yelled, but the nail didn't budge. It was really stuck! Now I wasn't sure what to do. We were standing there thinking and looking at each other, when Stephen suddenly gasped and said, "That's not a nail. That's a fishhook!" In alarm, we realized that Stephen was right. It was a fishhook. We hadn't recognized this right away, because the hook was completely in her foot and all we could see was the end of it. Now Grace was even more frightened (and so were we). Trying to calm her, we assured her that everything would be okay. We decided to call Mom and Dad at the restaurant.

"I'm sorry, but there's no Harold or Rebekah Mally here," we heard after the clerk tried to page them. We figured that we would just have to wait until our parents arrived home. Grace was not in much pain as long as she kept perfectly still. A short time later, our parents pulled in the driveway, knowing nothing about the surprise that awaited them. Stephen and I went running outside to meet them and we were both talking at once. Immediately, they guessed that something was wrong.

"Grace has a fishhook in her foot," we said. "We can't get it out!"

After an evaluation of the problem, my parents took Grace to a medical care facility close to our house. The obvious difficulty with fishhooks is the barb on the end. Hooks may go in easily but then they are stuck. At the doctor's office they gave Grace some shots to numb the area. Then they pushed the hook all the way through so they could clip off the barb and pull out the hook.

Grace was soon running around again as usual, but that day we had a family talk about hooks. We discussed how there are many spiritual hooks and snares and traps of the enemy. Just like fishhooks, these may go in easily, but they are traps. They do not come out easily.

These unresolved problems in our life are like hooks. Once they are in, it is much more difficult to get rid of them. They are painful to remove. For example, it may be easy to tell your brother a lie or to speak

unkind words to your sister, but it's a lot harder to make it right.

So here is the first step:

Gain a Clear Conscience

Little sins that are never made right will affect us for the rest of our lives. If there are little offenses we have not taken care of, we have guilt which will be a hindrance in our relationship with God and others. Guilt does to relationships what injuries, handicaps, diseases, or poisons do to the body. They hinder the way it functions.

Why does the Bible Emphasize a Clear Conscience?

Because we have to stand before God — *"And herein do I exercise myself, to have always a conscience void of offense toward God and toward men."* (Acts 24:14-16)

To avoid failure — *"Holding faith, and a good conscience; which some having put away concerning faith have made shipwreck."* (I Tim. 1:19)

To maintain a good testimony — *"Having a good conscience; that, wheras they speak evil of you, as of evildoers, they may be ashamed that falsely accuse your good conversation in Christ."* (I Pet. 3:16)

There are three types of consciences:

A Good Conscience
A GUILTY CONSCIENCE and
A DEAD CONSCIENCE

A dead conscience is the worst. It results from going against your conscience so much that sin doesn't even bother you anymore. Each of us should desire to have a conscience that is as sensitive as possible. If you go back to someone and ask forgiveness, your conscience will become more sensitive. But if you are not willing to go back and make it right, you will desensitize your conscience. If you rationalize and think, "Oh, I don't need to!" then the next time you do something wrong, it won't bother you as much. A sensitive conscience is the mark of a mature Christian. (Heb. 5:13-14)

When I was nine years old, my dad led a Bible study about a clear conscience. I remember thinking, "I really want to have a clear conscience, and I know that I don't have one." Even though I desired a clear conscience, I didn't do anything about it. Several years later, I realized that it was my responsibility to clear my conscience and ask forgiveness from those whom I had wronged. I made a list of all the people I had offended, and, one by one, began to ask their forgiveness. Not only did this strengthen my relationship with these people, it also strengthened my relationship with the Lord. Often the things that are the most difficult to do bring us the greatest joy and rewards.

DEAD CONSCIENCE	GUILTY CONSCIENCE	CLEAR CONSCIENCE
EVERYTHING SEEMS O.K.	DISCOMFORT AND FEAR	HUMBLE CONFESSION
"I didn't do it!"	"Who? Me? (gulp) No, um, I didn't do it."	"I'm sorry. It's my fault. I did it."

How to Clear Your Conscience

1. **List the offenses you have committed against your brothers and sisters** (actually, you should list everybody, but you can start with your brothers and sisters because that is what this book is about).

   Ask yourself:
   • "How did I offend them?"
   • "What were my wrong attitudes?"
   • "What were my wrong words and actions?"
   • "How did this hurt them?"

2. **Confess your sins to the Lord.** (I John 1:9)
   After you talk to the Lord about the problem, He often makes your sin clearer and enlightens you further. Then you have greater understanding to talk to your siblings about it.

3. **Purpose to ask forgiveness from those you have offended.**
   It is easy to rationalize and try to argue with yourself why you don't need to clear your conscience. Stephen's section has further insights on this.

4. **Determine when you will ask forgiveness and do it.**
   Decide now when the best time would be. Do not put it off.

5. **Show sincerity and humility when asking forgiveness.**
   When you ask forgiveness, your words must show true repentance. Be sure to take the blame yourself. Plan your words in advance. Grace's section will give you ideas about how to word this properly.

Yes, asking forgiveness is very hard to do, but remember that fishhooks do not come out easily. No matter how difficult, we must learn to maintain a clear conscience on an everyday basis with our brothers and sisters. Stephen, Grace, and I are learning how important this is.

Another helpful strategy is to look at these offenses from the other person's viewpoint. How did they feel? In what way were they injured by me? What were their losses or felt losses? Then tell them the answers to these questions so that they know we understand our error. What looks like something small in our eyes may look very big to someone else. Matthew 6:4-5 says that we should fix the big problems in our lives before we try to fix the small problems in someone else's life.

I remember one particular afternoon when Grace and I had a conflict. To set the scene for you, it was a very busy day; I had just finished writing a new harp trio and was very anxious to have Stephen and Grace try it with me. I was thrilled because Stephen agreed to practice the first time I asked him. The two of us came into the living room and told Grace that now was the only time we had to practice. Grace said that she was busy and asked if we could do it later.

I said, "No, we need to practice right now." She again explained that now was not a good time.

I answered, "We need to do this, Grace. Even Mom said we should practice now." After insisting that we had to do it immediately, Grace finally gave in. However, she wasn't very happy about it, and was causing trouble and trying to be a nuisance throughout the piece. When we ended, she went running downstairs, making it clear that she was very upset with me.

My first thought was that this problem was definitely not my fault. I had not become upset with her or said anything wrong. As I thought about it, I wondered what I should do, because I knew she was mad at me and I didn't want to leave it that way. I decided that I would try to look at this situation from her perspective. Immediately, the Lord convicted me that, although I had not responded unkindly, I had provoked her to anger. By getting the rest of the family on my side (they all agreed that we should practice), I had put her in a difficult situation and forced her to comply. I was not sensitive to her feelings, or concerned that I had caused her to stumble. Now I easily understood why she was upset with me.

After I recognized this, I went downstairs, explained this to her, and asked her to forgive me. She immediately forgave me and asked if I would forgive her. The problem was solved just like that, and no "unwanted strangers" (such as anger or bitterness) were left to grow into further problems.

The benefits of a clear conscience far outweigh the difficulty of obtaining one. Here are some of the benefits:

- You will be able to resolve conflicts.
- You will start this relationship with a fresh start and a clean slate.
- You will experience great freedom and joy (just imagine—no guilt!)
- You will receive excellent practice in humility.
- You will have more strength to overcome future temptations. (Next time you are tempted to do the same thing, you will remember how hard it is to ask forgiveness.)
- You will have boldness in your witness because your life will be free from hypocrisy.
- You will have a good testimony to others.

*"For our rejoicing is this, the **testimony of our conscience**, that in simplicity and godly sincerity, not with fleshly wisdom, but by the grace of God, we have had our conversation [behavior] in the world, and more abundantly to you-ward."* (II Cor. 1:12)

STEPHEN'S SECTION

The Battle Rages Within

To continue the thrilling episode about the attack of the comforter (page 86) ... As you may remember, our morning didn't have the greatest start. After our battle on the bed, Grace was abnormally silent. (Believe me, that is abnormal.) Neither of us felt like talking to the other person. As a result, the house was very peaceful—outwardly, that is. Inwardly, there was a war going on—between my mind and myself. My mind was losing; "myself" was winning (or something like that). Finally, I decided that I needed to do something about this problem, even if it wasn't totally my fault. So I walked into the living room where Grace was sitting. It wasn't exactly the place I felt like being at that moment. I told Grace that I was wrong to have gotten mad at her. (After all, she was just trying to play around.) I asked her if she would forgive me. She said, "Yes," and then asked me to forgive her. (And I, being the shrewd businessman that I am, said, "For a price!" Well, not really.)

Why did I feel that I needed to do something about our little fight? I mean, it wasn't a big deal, was it? Why couldn't I just forget about it? That was precisely the problem. I couldn't forget about it because of this thing called a conscience. People say that your conscience is something that always gets in the way. (And I would tend to agree with them.) When God created us He installed an auto guilt-detector. We shouldn't look at it as something bad. We need to pay attention when it signals that something is wrong.

So, your conscience is telling you that something is wrong. At the very same time, your mind tries to tell you that it wasn't your fault. Yet if it wasn't your fault, then why do you feel this way? Why do you have to think of reasons why it wasn't your fault? So, your next idea is to say that it was only 15% your fault. Well, do you want to stand before God and be 15% guilty for not having a good relationship with your brothers and sisters?

Then as a last resort, your mind begins to fire a whole bunch of reasons why you really don't need to clear your conscience. "It happened a long time ago." "I wouldn't want to remind them." "They might have forgotten." "Things have gotten better since then." "Maybe it was all just a dream." "It's physically impossible for me to do." "They will lose their respect for me." The mind can make a never-ending list of excuses.

Now it's time to face the truth. You need to go to the offended person and ask their forgiveness, but not just for 15%, not even for 99%. You need to claim all the responsibility. There is a good chance that after you humble yourself and take the blame (even the part you don't deserve), they will also ask you to forgive them. But of course, this should not be your motivation.

Okay, you have finally decided to do it and your mind comes up with one last tactic. "Now is not the best time." (The scientific term for this is procrastination.) This obstacle may be the biggest of all. Your mind tries to convince you, "They must be busy, so I'll do it later," or "It's a good thing they aren't home right now." But you need to pick a time and then do it. We shouldn't pick next year or at midnight when they're sleeping. Yes, it's nice, perhaps, to catch them in a good mood, but don't postpone it until Christmas Day after they've opened all their presents. And definitely, don't just say, "I'll do it later." Later never comes. It should be right away. When something is urgent, like your house is burning down, you don't say, "Someday I need to call the fire department," or "The fire department is probably busy right now. I wouldn't want to bother them."

Stephen's Definitions

Answers — What we have for other people's problems.

Popularity — Knowing that there are two sides to every question and taking both of them.

Conscience — Something that keeps more people awake than coffee.

Clear Conscience — Often the sign of a bad memory.

Problems — Psychiatrists tell us that talking solves these—it also causes them.

Eraser — The perfect invention for human beings.

Mind — A high tech, fully automated, non-battery-operated excuse maker (now with more memory!).

GRACE'S SECTION

I Made a Mistake, Now What?

"Why did I say that?" I asked myself.

"I know I shouldn't have told that story and now I feel guilty. Do I have to tell Stephen what I said about him? He's not going to like it. Why did I have to say it in the first place?"

These thoughts ran through my mind as I was at a friend's house. I had told a funny story about Stephen. I thought it was funny at the time, but I knew that if Stephen had heard what I had said, he wouldn't have liked it.

I called Sarah and told her the whole story. I asked her what I should do, and she said that I should probably tell Stephen. That is not exactly what I wanted to hear. So I explained to my friends that I shouldn't have said what I did about Stephen; I told them that I was going to ask his forgiveness when I got home.

I was not looking forward to asking Stephen's forgiveness. I thought he'd probably be upset, but I knew I didn't have a choice. I didn't want anything between us, hurting our relationship. And I knew that even if Stephen never found out, God knew what I said. I was a little nervous, but I realized that I had to do it.

First, I kind of "pre-warned" him. I said, "Um, Stephen, um, um, I, um, you see, I said something I shouldn't have yesterday ... I hope you won't be too upset ..." I told him the whole story and asked his forgiveness. Although I could tell he wasn't very happy at first, he was very forgiving.

Although This is Hard, It is Important!

Clearing your conscience is probably the hardest thing we write about in this book, but it is also one of the most important things. If Jenny's brothers (chapter four) had told her they were sorry for how they hurt her, and asked her forgiveness when it happened, there would be no problem now.

We want to have a totally pure conscience before the Lord. I know this is a hard chapter to read. Sometimes I will realize I need to clear my conscience, and I will be so afraid it gives me a stomachache. I just feel so scared and so terrible. I understand how hard it can be, but pray and ask the Lord for strength. *"It is God that girdeth me with strength, and maketh my way perfect."* (Ps. 18:32)

Don't Put It Off!

My dad had one younger brother. His name was Chuck. My dad told me that when he was younger, he didn't treat Chuck very well. As my dad grew older, he began to feel badly about how he had treated him. He decided he should talk to him about it, but he just didn't know how.

"Nobody ever does this," my dad thought. I think one problem was that nobody ever taught my dad how to clear his conscience when he was little.

Finally, my dad was just getting to the place where he was going to talk to Chuck. But then, Chuck died. You see, he had leukemia. It was too late and my dad was never able to ask his forgiveness.

Do It and Do It Right!

These are some of the **wrong ways** to ask for forgiveness:
- "I was wrong, but you were wrong, too."
- "If I was wrong, I'm sorry."
- "Since you get offended so easily, I guess I'll have to ask your forgiveness."
- "Sorry."
- "It wasn't my fault, but I'm sorry you got hurt."

When we go to our siblings and ask forgiveness, we must have the right attitude. We should show humility and take all the blame ourselves. This is hard, especially if you feel that you were mostly right and they were wrong.

Before you ask forgiveness, plan in advance how you will word it. Explain what you did wrong, with no mention of what they did. The best way is usually to admit, "I was wrong," and ask, "Will you forgive me?"

HIS STORY APPLIED TODAY

Well, I'll Forgive You Once More

Have you ever wondered if we need to keep forgiving those who hurt us? What if they do the same thing to us over and over? Peter came to Jesus one day asking that very question. "How about seven times?" Peter suggested. "Is that enough?" Jesus explained that he should forgive not just seven times, but seventy times seven. Jesus told him this story.

A certain king wanted to take account of his servants. One servant was brought to him which owed him ten thousand talents. Since the servant was not able to pay, the king commanded that he be sold along with his wife, children, and all that he had, so payment could be made. The servant was very distraught. He fell down and begged for more time, reassuring the king that he would pay it all. Amazingly, the king had compassion on the servant, set him free, and completely forgave him.

After he had been forgiven this enormous debt, this servant did something that is hard to believe. He went out and found another servant who owed him a mere hundred pence (not very much). He demanded that the money be paid immediately. Now this servant began to beg for mercy, but the first servant would show no compassion. Instead, he threw him into prison. When the king heard about this, he was furious. He called the first servant to him and said, *"O thou wicked servant, I forgave thee all that debt, because thou desiredst me: Shouldest not thou also have had compassion on thy fellowservant, even as I had pity on thee?"* He delivered him to the tormentors, until he should pay all that was due unto him. (You can read this story yourself in Matthew 18:21-35.)

It's unbelievable that this servant would act in this way, but I fear that many of us are just like that wicked servant. We have been forgiven a huge debt, and yet we refuse to forgive brothers and sisters who hurt us. We sinned against our Creator. He was willing to forgive us, even though it cost Him His Son, the Lord Jesus Christ. Any wrong that one of our brothers or sisters has done to us is nothing at all in comparison to the wrong that we have done to the Lord. We are commanded to forgive in this same immeasurable way that He has forgiven us.

"But God commendeth his love toward us, in that, while we were yet sinners, Christ died for us." (Rom. 5:8)

I'M PERPLEXED...

Question: I'm always the one picked on, how should I respond?

Answer: A little boy I know was in this situation. He was always picked on by his older brother. No matter what he did, his older brother seemed to constantly find fault, criticize, and make fun of him. Their fighting was mostly the older brother's fault but the younger brother made it worse by his reactions. He would get mad back, kick, punch, and call his brother names. This caused the older brother to tease him even more.

It is not "fun" to tease a person who doesn't react or yell back. One person cannot have a very interesting argument by himself. If you respond with humility and kindness, this will be an unexpected turn of events for your sibling.

I also encourage you to have a talk with your sibling about this. They may not realize how you feel. Choose a good time for this—when they are not upset. Explain the situation to them from your perspective; do not blame them, but instead ask them if there is anything you have been doing that aggravates them. (Warning: before you do this, read page 210 about how to receive a rebuke.)

Self-Evaluation Quiz 5

1. **I will forgive my brother...**
   - ☒ Unconditionally.
   - ❑ Seventy times seven times.
   - ❑ Only if he gets on his knees and begs humbly.
   - ❑ After the rapture.

2. **Asking my siblings to forgive me...**
   - ❑ Is something I might do ... sometime ... maybe.
   - ❑ Is as painful as pulling out a fishhook.
   - ❑ Is more scary than roller coasters.
   - ☒ Is a great way to practice humility.
   - ❑ Don't mention that, it makes me feel uncomfortable.
   - ❑ No comprendo.

3. **When my brother/sister talks, I...**
   - ❑ Look for earplugs.
   - ☒ Pretend I'm listening, while I plan my bedtime snack and wonder what I'll do tomorrow.
   - ❑ Exit the room as quickly as possible.
   - ❑ Stick a caramel apple in their mouth.
   - ❑ Imagine what it might be like to be deaf.
   - ☒ Smile, listen, and nod.

4. **I am willing to humbly receive advice and even "rebukes" from my brother/sister.**
   - ❑ Yes.
   - ☒ I try to.
   - ❑ I'll think about it.
   - ❑ Not a chance.
   - ❑ Next question, please.
   - ❑ You've gotta be kidding.

5. When my sister hits me, my normal response is to...
- ❑ "Fight the good fight" as literally as possible.
- ❑ Write her a ten page essay on the importance of a clear conscience.
- ❑ Pull the fire alarm.
- ❑ Turn the other cheek.
- ❑ Find a book on family warfare.
- ❑ Plan a sneak revenge attack when our parents aren't home.

6. When I'm on a family vacation and everyone is tired of traveling, the best way to respond to grouchy siblings is...
- ❑ Keep my head out the window.
- ❑ Play tic-tac-toe. Again. Again. Again.
- ❑ Pretend to be asleep.
- ❑ Experiment to see if I can change everyone else's attitude by being cheerful.
- ❑ Be grouchy, too, just to fit in.
- ❑ Ask them to teach me a class in Crabbiness 101.

CHAPTER SIX

Home Survival Kit

The Number One Key to All Relationships

SARAH'S SECTION

The Number One Key to All Relationships

Have you ever forgotten something really important? Have you ever **known** the answer about how to deal with a problem, but forgotten to use it when you needed it?

One Sunday morning, things at our house were going according to their normal routine. As it was getting close to the time to leave for church, Dad stepped outside to put something into the car. He was surprised that the car was not in the driveway. He walked out to the street. He hadn't remembered parking it there. It was unusual to do that. What he wasn't prepared for was the discovery that there was **no car** in the street. A rare chill quickly ran through him, as the only logical explanation dawned on him—theft. Nothing like this had ever happened before. He didn't know how to react or what to do. He came back in the house to tell Mom and decide the next step.

For a moment, they both sat there, stunned by this shocking reality. Then, before calling the police, it came to one of them to ask, "When did we have it last?" Neither could at first remember. They rehearsed the events of the night before. After shopping, they had met another couple at K-Mart and gone out to dinner together for their anniversary. After dinner the other couple dropped them off at home ... Can you believe it? They forgot the car at K-Mart. Sometimes people misplace their keys, but our parents misplaced their car. Now they had two problems: how to get to church and how to get their car!

In the same way, have you ever forgotten an item, and therefore faced disaster or loss? Have you ever looked back and wondered how you could be so foolish, or how you could have forgotten something so important? Many times we have all the knowledge we need to come up with a solution, but we do not use what we know.

There is a key, a "Number One Key," to all relationships, that people often forget. Everyone has heard about it. We all know we should do it, but it doesn't come to our mind when we have the opportunity. If people would just remember to apply this one key, almost all of their relationship troubles would be solved. If there were such a thing as a magic formula that would cure all problems in getting along, this would be it.

Jesus demonstrated this key more fully than anyone else ever has. David, Abraham, John the Baptist, Esther, Isaac, Paul, Mary Magdalene, the centurion in Matthew chapter eight, and others also found this key to be vital.

If you're not sure what this key is, maybe Grace's quiz will help you figure it out:

What Am I?

- "Using me, it is possible to get along with almost anyone.
- Many great kings despised me, but the greatest One loved me.
- If brothers and sisters demonstrate me daily, their relationships will greatly improve.
- The Bible says to be 'clothed' with me. (1 Pet. 5:5)
- Marriages have been broken because they neglected me.
- Whoever receives me will be exalted, and will receive grace. (I Pet. 5:5-6)
- Fights have lasted a lifetime because people rejected me.
- By the fear of the Lord and me, are riches, honor and life. (Prov. 22:4)
- One man refused me and therefore got dangers, terrors, problems, embarrassment, and terrible consequences. (Ex. 5-11)
- Churches have been split because they forgot about me.

What am I?"

By Grace

This amazing key is called humility.

"Yea, all of you be subject one to another, and be clothed with humility: for God resisteth the proud, and giveth grace to the humble. Humble yourselves therefore under the mighty hand of God, that He may exalt you in due time." (I Pet. 5:5-6)

"Before destruction the heart of man is haughty, and before honor is humility." (Prov. 18:12)

Be the Least

The word humility comes from the word "**dirt**" (humus). We could think of it, therefore, as "putting yourself below and underneath," or "giving the other person the upper position." To the world, this key sounds like absolute foolishness. The world tells us to stand up for our rights and not to let others push us around, but God's ways are opposite to man's ways. It is the one who is humble who exhibits true strength. The one who is willing to be the loser is the sure winner. Jesus says,

"Whosoever, therefore, shall humble himself as this little child, the same is greatest in the kingdom of heaven." (Matt. 18:4)

It is incredible how God's ways always work. Try this key called humility and you will be amazed at the results. Let me give you a few examples:

Example # 1

When I was in second grade, before we began to homeschool, I was sitting at my desk at the Christian school. During school that day, my red pencil fell on the ground. Before I had a chance to pick it up, the girl sitting next to me reached down and took it. I asked for it back, but she told me that it was hers. That evening, when I came home, I told my mom about the problem. I thought my mom would talk to the teacher so I could get my pencil back, but instead, she suggested that I use this key called humility.

She told me, "Why don't you give your red pencil away to this girl? In fact," she said, "let's go to the store and buy a whole pack of pencils for you to give her." Mom and I picked out a pack of specially carved pencils.

The next day at school, instead of demanding my red pencil back, I handed this new pack of pencils to my friend and said, "I'd like to give you these." She was shocked. Suddenly I became her good friend. This small incident led to a nice friendship between us. Because of it, I had continued opportunities to minister to this girl and invest in her life. Looking back, I realized my mom was right. Humility worked!

Example # 2

A family we know was upset with us. Though we hadn't meant to do anything wrong, we had irritated them and caused them an inconvenience. Now they were upset. They wrote to us several times explaining how we had offended them and caused them so many difficulties. To solve the problem, they insisted that we comply with their request, and change the area of our life which bothered them. I didn't think we needed to submit to their demand (which required a sacrifice on our part that I was not too happy about). My parents, however, remembered this key called humility. They explained to us kids that we were not going to argue, but simply, "let them win." We did this, but we were not expecting their change of attitude which followed. It was incredible! Instead of treating us like an irritation in their life, they treated us like their best friends. They bragged to others about how wonderful we were, and they catered to us kids as if we were in their family. This amazing key worked again!

Example # 3

A great leader had been deeply offended by a wicked man. He was angry, and was on his way to destroy this wicked man who offended him (as well as his household). This wicked man happened to have a godly wife and she heard about the trouble their household was in. This godly woman applied humility to the situation. She came to this great leader and fell on her face before him. She brought him gifts, and humbly said that she would take all the blame for this situation. Her humility saved her entire household, and also protected this leader from a foolish decision. In the days that followed, God blessed this woman. Her name was Abigail. You can read the story in I Samuel 25.

I could give you many more examples of how this key works. God opposes the proud, but He gives grace to the humble. Unfortunately, death to pride is the hardest death to die. It is like spiritual cancer that is deeply rooted within each one of us.

For Christmas one year, Stephen and I received a hockey game. (It was like a small foosball game.) We played it often and had a great time together, but one night we had a fight.

"Stephen, that's not fair!"

"Yes, it is."

"Stephen, you always cause trouble when you start to lose. You have to play according to the rules."

"I **am** playing according to the rules. You're the one who isn't."

"Yes, I am! But Stephen, you can't do that."

"Well, I'm quitting then."

"You always give up when things don't go your way!"

"Sarah, I do not!"

"Hey, put that hockey puck back."

"No."

"Well, I'll take it from you then."

At this point, I grabbed the hockey puck from Stephen. (I, being bigger than him, had the advantage. Things have changed since then. Little brothers grow.) I captured the puck and ran to my desk. I was sitting there feeling upset. "Stephen is not being fair," I thought to myself. "I'm not going to let him get away with it this time."

One of us needed to show humility. As long as we continued in our pride, we would stubbornly stand up for ourselves and not give in. As I was sitting there at my desk, I knew I had not handled the situation correctly. I knew that I was the oldest one, and that instead of waiting for him to say he was sorry, I needed to clear up my part of the problem. With reluctance, I decided that I would be the first one to admit my fault and apologize. After I was willing to humble myself, Stephen was willing to humble himself, too.

How To Apply Humility

Make the decision that you will take the humble position in your family. This is difficult to do, but God will reward you. Starting today, look for opportunities to humble yourself with your brothers and sisters. Here are some possible ways:

- Be willing to listen to them instead of talking about yourself.
- Ask for their help and advice.
- Consider your siblings more important than yourself (Phil. 2:3-4).
- Be willing to do things their way. Don't make all the decisions. (This is especially hard for firstborns.)
- Let others be the first to tell the latest news.
- Say, "I was wrong," and explain why.
- Ask forgiveness.
- Share your struggles.
- Be quick to give in when there is a problem.
- Never put them down by joking about them.
- Express gratefulness and thankfulness for the ways they benefit your life.
- Be willing to do the things no one else wants to do.
- Look for ways to serve them.
- Submit to them (Ephesians 5:21).
- Try to fit into their schedule, rather than forcing them to fit into yours.
- Let them have the best (places to sit, things to eat, things to have, etc.).
- Let them win the argument.
- Don't defend yourself when they criticize you.

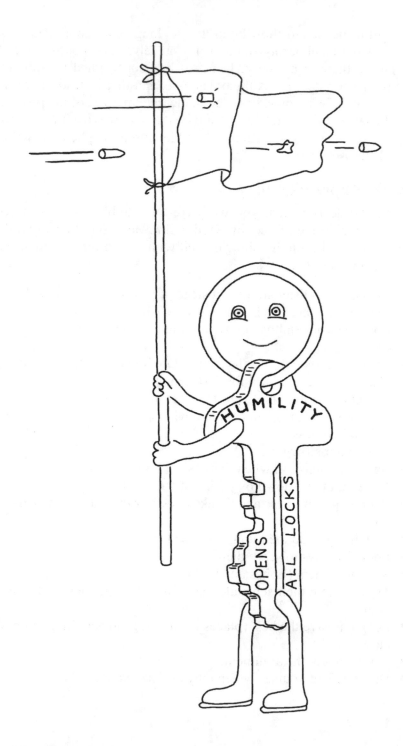

STEPHEN'S SECTION

A Universal Problem, A Universal Key

Sarah told you about the time my parents lost their car, so I thought I'd tell you about the time my parents lost their key. We arrived home, in the middle of the night, after a long trip. As usual, we were anxious to get out of our car and into our home sweet home. That's when we made a tragic discovery. We didn't have our own house key. Can you believe it? Neither can I. We were stuck in our van, in the middle of the night, wondering what to do. We decided that we'd have to wake up our friends who had been watching our house. This we did, only to discover that they had locked the key inside our house only hours before. Now our options were to break into our own house, to unpack the entire van in the driveway and search for our key, or to stay in the van and freeze. What would you do?

I assume that you have the key to your house, but do you have the key to your home? Do you know the key to having a close relationship with your family? More importantly, are you using the key? This key, as you already know, is humility.

I'm Sure I'm Right

Let's see here, I need to think of an example of pride. I know, I'll tell you a story about my sisters. One day Sarah and Grace were planning a surprise for my mom and the two of them were on their way to prepare for it. Unfortunately, when they were just about to leave the house, Grace accidentally "let the cat out of the bag." As Sarah and Grace got into the van to leave, they both agreed that the surprise was ruined. Sarah was not too happy that Grace had blown the secret after they had gone to all that work to keep it a surprise.

As Sarah was driving, she thought to herself, "I'm not going to criticize Grace. I don't know why she was so careless, but I won't tell her how upset I am. I don't want to hurt her feelings, so I just won't say anything at all."

Now at the same time, Grace was in the other seat thinking, "Why isn't Sarah comforting me? Doesn't she know that I feel bad about it, too? Why did she have to agree with me that the surprise was ruined? Why is she just clamming up? She sure doesn't know the right way to treat someone who is sad." (So, how do I know all this? No, I can't read people's minds—especially my sisters'! I just happen to have my spies everywhere.)

When Sarah and Grace arrived, Sarah was shocked to find that Grace was upset with her. After all, she had thought she had gone out of her way to be nice. The two of them were looking at the situation completely differently and they both thought they were right! That is how pride gets in the way. You think you are right and you don't want to accept the fact that someone else might be. Humility is putting others above yourself.

Now, let's say I walk up to Grace and tell her something. Then let's say Grace interrupts and corrects me, and explains that I am mistaken. I can't let her be right. Why? Because if she is right, then I am wrong. That would hurt my pride. I have something to lose, you see, and my pride gets in the way.

Don't underestimate pride. In fact, let me warn you of another thing to be careful about when you begin to apply humility. Sometimes you will discover that you are proud because you are so humble. Pride is very subtle. It creeps in all over the place. We can often see pride in other people, but we can rarely see it in ourselves. To help us evaluate ourselves, let's list some of the symptoms of pride:

- Not wanting to ask forgiveness
- Always having to stand up for our rights
- Always defending ourselves
- Wanting everyone to think well of us
- Insisting on doing something our own way
- Thinking that we are more important than other people
- Needing to prove that we were right
- Not wanting to admit that someone else knew something that we didn't
- Not being able to accept criticism
- Being happy when someone else fails
- Being glad when we are better than others

HARMFUL WORDS

Stephen's Definitions

Public Opinion — What people think people think.

Mistakes — Something made only by others; we only make unavoidable errors.

Faults — When looking for these, use a mirror, not a telescope.

Argument — When two people are trying to get in the last word first.

Key Ring — A device that enables you to lose several keys at the same time.

Justice — Any decision made in my favor.

GRACE'S SECTION

No More Fights!

Think back to the last argument or fight you had with a sibling. Okay, do you remember it? Now, I will tell you *why* you had your problem. You say, "What do you mean, you will tell me? Even I don't know why it happened!" Well, I *do* know! ... It happened because of PRIDE! The Bible says, *"Only by pride cometh contention."* (Prov. 13:10)

So, we want humility, right? What is humility? It is lowering yourself. It is taking the blame. It is being able to say, "It was my fault." The reason this is important in families is because humility will prevent arguments and fights. (Or, if you decide to start showing humility halfway through your fight, it will stop it then, too.)

Of course, all brothers and sisters will disagree with each other here and there (or everywhere). Disagreeing isn't sin, like being tempted isn't sin. Even Jesus was tempted and He was perfect! The trouble starts when we let ourselves begin arguing. And the reason we start arguing or fighting is because of pride! And the reason we don't show humility more is because we want our way, and it's too hard to say, "I was wrong."

⊗ ⊛
IMPORTANT NOTICE
TO OLDER SIBLINGS:
1. Don't read the following paragraph!
2. Or if you do, please forget it afterwards, and don't have any expectations.
⊕ ⊕

Advice to Younger Ones

Giving in during an argument isn't the only way to show humility. Another way to show humility is by serving your brothers and sisters, instead of trying to boss them around. You may be thinking, "Be a servant? ... To my older brothers and sisters? ... Are you kidding?" No, I'm not kidding. As the younger sibling, don't try to "take over" (if that is possible!) and get them to do what you want. Instead, try being their servant. Assist them in their work. Ask if they need help. Don't insist on doing it your way.

Now Sarah is probably telling the older brothers and sisters not to be bossy, but instead, to serve. I think that's great! But I think we younger ones should decide that we will serve them anyway.

I used to ask Sarah to do things for me all the time. "Sarah, my pencil broke. Would you mind getting me another one?" or "Sarah, could you finish the dishes for me? I want to go play!" or "Wait for me! I just have to get my socks and shoes!" Sarah was always a very nice big sister so she would do it, but now that we've talked about it, I've found out that it was a big irritation to her. I didn't realize or see this at the time, but now as I look back I see how she must have felt. I was not being a servant.

The best way to learn humility is to follow the example of Jesus. Even though He is King of kings and Lord of lords, Creator of the universe, He came down as a little baby to earth. He was not born in a king's palace, but placed in a manger where animals eat! Throughout His whole life on earth, we see how humble Jesus was. Finally, He was crucified on a cross with criminals! Jesus took all the blame for the sins of all the human beings that ever lived, and that ever will live on the earth! Jesus was the only One who **didn't** deserve the punishment!

If Jesus showed so much humility, shouldn't we be humble with our siblings and take the blame even when we don't deserve it?

THE BETHLEHEM STABLE

Deflecting Praise

One more way to express humility is to deflect praise. Everyone gets compliments or praise at one time or another. That's a good thing, but most of the time, we are not the ones who are responsible for the success. After all, God gave us life and strength and skill. Our parents took care of us and taught us and protected us. Actually, everything we have was given to us. So if we take all the glory ourselves, it is like saying, "Thanks! I'm glad you noticed how great I am." But if we tell them where our ability really came from, and that it is actually not ours, we are being humble and passing the credit on to the one it belongs to.

There was a girl about my age who stayed with our family for a few days. She had a little brother and a little sister. I noticed that whenever her little sister or brother wanted something, or needed help, she was always helping them. She seemed to do more for them than for herself! I was impressed with how patient and kind she was to them. When I told her that I noticed this, she deflected the praise to Christ and said, "Well, thank you, it is the Lord that really gives me the strength to be kind to them!"

Here's an example of deflecting praise. Let's say that your parents bought you a piano. They paid for your piano lessons, helped you learn your pieces, reminded you to practice each day, and encouraged you. If someone comes over and tells you that you play nicely, should you get all the credit? One way you could deflect praise would be by saying, "Thank you, my parents have helped me a lot."

I'M PERPLEXED...

Question: If I take the humble position, they will think that they are right, and can always get their way, won't they?

Answer: It may seem that way. But there are two things you need to realize. The first thing is that God opposes the proud but gives grace to the humble. (I Pet. 5:5) God will exalt you in His time and it is His responsibility to take care of their pride. Is there anyone better to have on your side than God?

The second thing to realize is that your godly response will be a surprise to them. Your humble attitude will disarm them. If you stubbornly insist on your own way, you will push them to become stronger in their position; but if you humble yourself, you will find that this is the best way to influence them to do the same.

HIS STORY APPLIED TODAY

Great Men Are Not So Great

The best way to get this chapter on humility in perspective is to get a glimpse of the greatness of God. We will quickly be humbled when we think of the incredible God we serve. He is the King of Kings and the Lord of Lords! Therefore, let's consider how a few faithful men responded when they came into the presence and greatness of God. These were some of the greatest men of God in all of history.

- **Job** is honored in Scripture as a perfect and upright man who feared the Lord and hated evil. In Job 1:8, God Himself says, *"There is none like him in the earth."* Yet after the Lord spoke to him (Job 38-41), Job's response was, *"I abhor myself, and repent in dust and ashes."* (Job 42:6)

- **Isaiah** was a great prophet of the Lord, but in the presence of God he said, *"Woe is me! For I am undone, because I am a man of unclean lips, and I dwell in the midst of a people of unclean lips: for mine eyes have seen the King, the Lord of Hosts."* (Is. 6:5)

- **Daniel** is one whom we all admire for his courage, convictions, and dedication to God. But when he saw a vision of the Lord, he said, *"There remained no strength in me: for my comeliness has turned in me into corruption, and I retained no strength ... and when I heard the voice of His words, then was I in a deep sleep on my face, and my face toward the ground."* (Dan. 10:8-9)

- **John the Baptist** was chosen by God to prepare the way for the Messiah, yet he acknowledged that he was not even worthy to untie Jesus' sandals. (Matt. 3:11)

- **John the disciple** spent much time with Jesus on earth, and was one of His closest friends, but when He beheld the Lord Jesus in glory, he said, *"When I saw Him, I fell at His feet as dead."* (Rev. 1:17)

These were great men of God; they were some of the best. Yet these men realized that, in God's presence, all of their greatness was completely inadequate. If they were inadequate, what about us? We ought to be utterly humble. But we are able to rejoice because our righteousness is completely and only in Christ—the One who is adequate. Therefore, we fall before Christ in total, humble dependence.

Self-Evaluation Quiz 6

1. I show humility when...
- ❑ My brother's not home.
- ❑ I'm not home.
- ❑ I'm in my room and the door is locked.
- ☑ I remember that I'm trying to please the Lord and not impress people.
- ☑ There's no other option.
- ❑ I'm losing in arm wrestling.

2. I greet my brother/sister with an enthusiastic smile and welcome...
- ❑ Always.
- ☑ Sometimes.
- ☑ When I'm in a good mood.
- ❑ Rarely.
- ❑ When things are going right for me that day.
- ❑ When they are bringing ice cream to share.
- ❑ After they have done the same to me.

3. I ask forgiveness when I have wronged my brother/sister...
- ❑ Never.
- ❑ Occasionally.
- ☑ Consistently.
- ❑ In the desperate situations.
- ❑ I will, before I die.

4. A typical response when my sister yells at me is to...
- ❑ Cover her mouth with duct tape.
- ❑ Find earmuffs.
- ❑ Practice an emergency get away.
- ❑ Find a megaphone and respond forcefully.
- ❑ Apply Matthew 5:3-12.
- ❑ Slowly leave the room.

5. When my sister and I are both trying to use the bathroom mirror at the same time, the best response is...

❑ In humility, to prefer others before myself.

❑ In pride, to prefer myself before others.

❑ To get my brother to be judge between us.

❑ To knock at my neighbor's door and request to use their bathroom mirror.

CHAPTER SEVEN

Oh Brother!

Dealing with "Bothers" and Sisters

SARAH'S SECTION

Dealing with "Bothers" and Sisters

Sarah: I think we should begin this chapter with personal examples of irritations from our family.

Stephen: VETOED. I don't think that's a good idea. For one thing, older sisters always use their younger brothers and sisters for their stories and illustrations. They also tend to make younger brothers and sisters look stupid.

Grace: I agree with Stephen. One hundred percent!

Sarah: Well, then, how should we begin this chapter? If you don't like my idea, why don't you give me some ideas of your own?

Grace: Well, you never like our ideas anyway, so why even give them to you?

Stephen: I agree with Grace. One hundred percent!

Sarah: Okay, let's just start with some personal testimonies then.

Stephen: No, we already decided against that.

Sarah: We?

Stephen: Oh, excuse me, the majority did.

Grace: Somehow, Sarah thinks that since she's the oldest, she gets to make all the decisions.

Sarah: Somehow, it seems that the oldest one does all the work.

Stephen: Personally, I think the oldest one does all the delegating.

Sarah: We're getting off the subject. How shall we start this chapter on irritations?

Grace: Let's do it later.

Sarah: No. We've got to get this book done.

Stephen: Why? Are you getting married soon?

Sarah: No, but let's keep working. If we don't start with stories, then how could we start?

Grace: Here we go again! You are so practical. By the way, you never even asked us if we wanted to work on the book right now.

Stephen: Yep, just like any other slave driver. Whose idea was this book, anyway?

Sarah: Come on, you guys. What can we write about irritations?

Grace: What are irritations?

Stephen: We never have them in our family. That's why you don't know what they are.

Grace: I know you are teasing me, Stephen! Why do you always do that?

Sarah: Listen, you two, are you going to help or not?

Stephen: We *are* helping!

Grace: Yeah, but Sarah, what are irritations? Stephen won't tell me.

Sarah: An irritation is when someone, *or two people,* are doing something that is bothering and aggravating you.

Stephen: Or it could be that they are SAYING something that is annoying you?

Grace: Or I suppose it could it be what they WON'T SAY to you?

Sarah: Yes, or it could be what they WON'T DO for you.

Stephen: It could also be what they are ASKING you to do.

Sarah: Or what they are saying ABOUT you.

Grace: I think I understand now, but maybe we should find a different author for this chapter ...

In a group of thousands of students, the question was asked, "How many of you are sometimes irritated by your brothers and sisters?" As I saw almost every student quickly raise his hand, it became very apparent to me that the problem of irritations is a universal one. When we spend day after day with the same people, we soon notice their character deficiencies, and they notice ours. Even if there are no big problems in our relationship, our brothers and sisters often annoy and aggravate us. Sometimes they do this on purpose; other times they don't even realize they're bothering us. Either way, the irritations build up and tend to get worse. As you are working through this book, trying to improve things in your family, you may find that irritations (which may seem small) can be your biggest hindrance.

I don't know what kinds of irritations you have in your family, but here are a few common ones:

- Someone who loses their temper.
- Someone who talks too much.
- Someone who won't talk or communicate.
- Someone who is always complaining.
- Someone who criticizes and finds fault instead of giving praise.
- Someone who is careless and breaks your things.
- Someone who always insists upon being right.
- Someone who has an endless list of questions to ask.
- Someone who nags.

- Someone who is messy and unorganized.
- Someone who is excessively neat and always putting away other people's things.
- Someone who is never ready to leave on time.
- Someone who doesn't help with things around the house.
- Someone who is a hypocrite (acts differently around other people than the family).
- Someone who is always touching your stuff.
- Someone who is constantly asking you to help them.
- Someone who is always bragging about themselves.

Irritations in Our Family

The Canine Tornado

My mom does not like dogs, especially not big ones, and *especially* not wild ones, and **especially** not in the house. One dark and stormy day we heard a knock on our door. Opening it, we saw a good friend. She looked rather frightened as she explained, "As I was driving by your house, I realized that there is a tornado watch. May I come inside until the storm is over?"

"Of course," we said, "Come right in."

"Oh, and can my dog come in, too?" she asked. We all looked at Mom.

"Um ... sure," Mom said. (What else could she say?) Just as Mom was looking out the door, hoping to see a tiny, calm dog ... What was that? Like a streak of lightning, in dashed a big, wet, wild dog. He began running laps through the house.

Since the storm was raging, we went to the basement for safety. We were all watching this dog that was now running laps around our basement. Unfortunately, our bed in the bedroom was part of his racetrack. Around and around he ran, past our conversation, through the bedroom, over the bed, and past us again. We were surprised that the lady didn't even seem to notice her dog. The rest of us sure noticed! We kept looking back and forth at the dog and at Mom's face; we couldn't decide which was more interesting to watch. I'll have to say that Mom's attitude toward dogs did not improve as a result of this experience.

It seemed like the longest tornado ever. The question is, "Was the tornado inside or outside?"

Hurry Up and Wait

Does it take your family a long time to pack for a trip? In our family, we have found that waiting for others is a frequent irritation. Because we are involved in a variety of ministry events, it sometimes seems like we are always packing or unpacking. Whenever we leave on a trip, we like to get up early so that we can get an early start. After our morning devotions, we eat breakfast and pack. But before we leave, we have to finish all uncompleted tasks that can't wait until we get back. Dad changes the oil in the car, while Mom packs the food and coffee. We cancel our music lessons and bread customers, and arrange for a neighbor to take out the garbage. We water the plants, turn down the heat, check e-mails, and say good-bye to our friends. Meanwhile, Mom wants to leave the house clean and neat. After everything is ready, then we wait for Dad and Grace. Grace makes sure she brings each of her stuffed animals, while Dad is sure to bring all of his journals, Bibles, and concordances. After the car is packed, the garage door shut, the lights off, the computer shut down, and the house locked, do you know what time it is? It is time to go to bed, so we can get up early and get an early start!

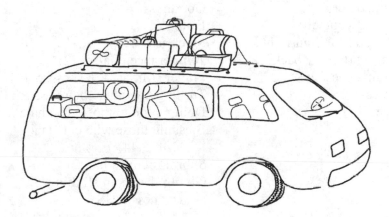

The Solution to the Irritation Dilemma

As much as we might like the idea, the solution to dealing with irritations is not to create an irritation-free environment. In our life we will always have irritations. God allows them for a reason. Therefore, the way to apply this chapter is **not** to get all irritations out of your life, because that would be impossible. Rather, it is to learn to respond properly to them.

If we had time to prepare for every situation and irritation, we would probably be able to determine how to respond correctly. But we rarely have that luxury. Something bothers us and without even thinking about it, we respond in a wrong way. No one has to teach us how to do this. It seems to happen automatically; it's like a reflex. We commonly rely on these natural human responses, which are always controlled by pride, selfishness, fear, jealousy, envy, and greed. We all know about physical reflexes. Well, there are also reflexes of our sinful nature, which the Bible refers to as the "flesh" (vs. the spirit). If we do not learn how to *"put off the old man [old self] which is corrupt"* (see Ephesians 4:22), we will continue to respond wrongly to the irritations God allows in our life. Our automatic reactions will control our decisions.

Responses of the Flesh:	**Responses of the Spirit:**
Jealousy	Love
Complaining	Joy
Arguing	Peace
Anger	Longsuffering
Being harsh and impatient	Gentleness
Blaming others	Goodness
Defending yourself	Faith
Standing up for your rights	Meekness
Disrespect (talking back/ rolling eyes/ etc.)	Temperance (Gal. 5:22)
	Prayer (Mt. 5:44, I Thess. 5:17)
Bitterness	Turning the other cheek (Mt. 5:39)
Silence	Doing good to those who hate us
	Blessing those who curse us (Mt. 5:44)
	Submission (Eph. 5:21)
	Giving thanks in all things (I Thess. 5:18)

Galatians 5:16 says, *"Walk in the Spirit, and ye shall not fulfill the lust of the flesh. For the flesh lusteth against the Spirit, and the Spirit against the flesh: and these are contrary the one to the other; so that ye cannot do the things that ye would."*

It is clear that the answer is to walk in the Spirit, not in the flesh. If certain irritations continue to overcome and defeat us so that we display responses of the flesh, it must be that we are **not** walking in the Spirit. This process of walking in the Spirit begins when we accept Christ as our

Savior and place our faith in Him. He gives us a new nature because the Holy Spirit indwells us. Our old selves are crucified with Him. Now it is our goal to have responses of the Spirit, rather than of the flesh, and, even more than that, our goal must be for these godly responses to become automatic (just as the flesh tends to be automatic).

We will only be able to have automatic godly responses as we employ Biblical tools. For instance, humility (chapter six) will disengage our pride and ulterior motives, self-control will keep our selfishness and greed in check, and sensitivity (chapter eight) will keep us focused on the other person instead of ourselves. To state it simply, this means that Jesus is on the throne in our heart and we are acting the way He would act. If Jesus is on the throne, then self must be on the cross.

"I am crucified with Christ: nevertheless I live; yet not I, but Christ liveth in me: and the life which I now live in the flesh I live by the faith of the Son of God, who loved me, and gave Himself for me." (Gal. 2:20)

"He that is slow to anger is better than the mighty; and he that ruleth his spirit than he that taketh a city." (Prov. 16:32)

Spiritual might is stronger than physical might!

How David Handled This Hindrance

King David was having one of the worst days of his life. His son, Absalom, had deceitfully tricked him and was trying to take over the kingdom. Now David was forced to flee for his life. In the midst of this turmoil, a man named Shimei came out and began to cast stones and dust at David, and to curse him and call him names. Surely this was a major irritation to David. David's servants were furious and asked him for permission to do away with this irritation, and take the head off Shimei. David, however, displayed a godly response by telling his servants that this irritation was from God, and that it was up to the Lord to take care of Shimei. David accepted this irritation as from the Lord, realizing that God was using this frustrating situation for good. (II Sam. 16:5-14)

So What Should I Do When My Brother is Bugging Me?

1. **Accept this irritation as from the Lord** (like David did). *Give thanks in everything.* (I Thess. 5:18, James 1:2-4).

2. **Examine yourself for what you may have done to cause this irritation.**

After examining yourself, make any changes in your life which may help to solve this problem.

3. Determine what you can learn through the irritation.
Look past your brother or sister or whoever is offending you. Look past whatever it is that they are doing and ask, "What is the Lord trying to teach me through this situation?" (Phil. 1:12-14, Gen. 50:20, and Rom. 8:28-29)

4. See his need.
Often those who cause pain for other people are the ones who are in the most desperate need for help themselves. Overcome evil with good by investing in their life. (See next chapter.)

5. View this as a test from the Lord.
As you purpose to apply this chapter, be prepared for the tests that God will bring. The way you respond often depends on how you look at things. When a difficult situation or an irritation arises, if you look at it as a "problem" or as "defeat," you will most likely respond wrongly by complaining and becoming angry. But if you look at it as a test from the Lord, you can be excited about how He is working in you. God gives us tests because He wants us to succeed and He wants to reward us. If we fail these tests, we miss out on the rewards He wants to give us. I encourage you to look forward with eager anticipation and excitement to your next test!

Some Examples of How This Has Worked:

Example # 1

Several years ago, I was annoyed with Grace because I felt that she was always asking me to do things for her. "Why can't she do these things herself?" I wondered. "Why is she always asking me?" One particular afternoon when she asked me to go downstairs and get something, I was especially annoyed. Outwardly, I tried to just do what she wanted, but inwardly, I was getting upset.

Then I stopped and asked the Lord, "How should I respond to this? What are you trying to teach me?" The Lord reminded me that I wanted to work on being a servant. He showed me that He was giving me a perfect opportunity to practice this. Then I realized, "Maybe the Lord is **having** Grace ask me to do things, **just** to teach me character and help me become a servant." I decided to delight in doing things for Grace. Guess what? Just a few days later, I noticed that Grace wasn't asking me to do things for her anymore!

Example # 2

A friend of mine had a problem with her younger brothers. They were constantly leaving **their** games on **her** bed. This young lady was confused about how to handle this irritating situation. Since she shared a room with her sisters, she didn't have much space to herself. Her bed was one thing that she liked to keep neat and clean. It was her own area. The problem was that her bed was near the closet where the family kept all their games. Her brothers would play these games and leave them on her bed, instead of putting them away. This was a continual irritation to her. She repeatedly asked her brothers to stop doing this, but it didn't seem to make any difference. What should she have done?

Finally, this friend decided that instead of trying to change her brothers, she would change her attitude about this irritation. She went to her brothers and said, "I want you to know that from now on, when you play those games, you can set them on my bed. Since you are not tall enough to put them away, just leave them there, and I will put them away for you." Now every night before she goes to bed, she puts the games away. This is a daily reminder to her of her love for her brothers. As she puts the games away, she also remembers that her bed and time are not hers anyway—they belong to the Lord.

STEPHEN'S SECTION

"Bothers?" and Sisters

First off, it should be very clear that I didn't name this chapter. I suppose if sisters think that brothers are sometimes "bothers," they might be right. Irritations, on the other hand, come in all shapes and sizes. (Many times, they look just like your sister!) So this chapter could also be called "Dealing with Irritations."

The first question that comes to my mind is, "Does this even matter? I mean, if people are irritating us, why do we have to worry about how we treat them? Don't they deserve to be irritated back?" Well, if God tells us to bless those who curse us, and love our enemies, I guess that also applies to those who irritate us. God wants us to have the right response to them.

The Explosion

So, what are irritations? Well, suppose a boy named Bobby walks over to his sister, Susie, and starts tapping her on the head. She tries to move so as to avoid him, but he keeps tapping her head. After five minutes, "Thar she blows." Why would this happen? Obviously, it was because Bobby was an irritation to her. But there are two sides to this. Even if tapping her on the head wasn't exactly the best thing to do, Susie still shouldn't blow her top. She ought to handle it in the right way. A person may respond properly outwardly (like for the first five minutes), but inwardly, get more and more upset. Watch out! Irritations will build up inside. We just hold it in ... hold it in ... and then it happens. We might not explode at first, but later on, something very small can tip the scale. So if your brother (or sister) is driving you nuts, and **inwardly**, you are stomping around and fuming, but **outwardly**, you pat the little "bother" on the head and tell him to have a nice day, beware of problems ahead. Improper inward reactions will explode.

Now "bothers" can be both male and female. The problem with "bothers" is that after they begin bugging you, your attitude toward them will change and you won't like anything about them. You will see everything they do as aggravating—how they talk, dress, walk, and even, sometimes, how or what they eat. These things can't be the real problem, because you know other people who do the same things, and you get along fine with them. So what is the real problem? First of all, it is that we are selfish and only thinking of our own interests. Secondly, an irritation often bothers us because it hinders us from reaching some desire that we have. Thirdly, we must remember that sometimes the problem is deeper than that (see chapter four). And finally, the fact that we may like other activities, have opposite interests, and have different strengths and weaknesses may also add to the problem.

The Days You'd Like to Forget

Have you ever had one of those days where everything is going wrong? You know, when you say to yourself, "I can't take this any longer. My sister is driving me up the wall. I can't stand this. I think I am going to go crazy!" It's on those kinds of days that it's hard to respond properly to irritations. And it's on days like that when the irritations keep coming and coming.

About five years ago, our family had an especially difficult Christmas. My grandmother was sick and we went to her house to help care for her. As a result, we were not able to do all the nice family things we look forward to doing during the Christmas season. To make matters worse, Grandma's house was extremely small and it was full to the brim. In fact, the house was so small, it was hard to even find a place to sit down.

A typical day at her house would be something like this: Mom would be asking me to do my school work, and it seemed like she was reminding me at least every five minutes. Grace had no place other than the living room to disperse her energy. She was quite the noisemaker back then. My grandmother was very sick and it was hard for her to be cheerful. Then Sarah would come to ask me to help move something, or to tell me of some great new idea she had. In the meantime, I would be looking for my pencil, so I could start my schoolwork. But how could I find anything with everyone's stuff all over? Besides, I had been waiting for the bathroom since 8:00 A.M. Is it possible to have correct responses on a day like that? Or with brothers and sisters who bug you constantly? Yes. Sarah gave some good answers, and don't forget James 1:2-4 which tells us that we can respond joyfully to trials because God gives rewards when we pass tests.

The key to dealing with "bothers" is to "overcome evil with good." Therefore, we need to praise, help, listen, pray, serve, and do kind things for them. We shouldn't tease, criticize, gossip about them, or blame them, or we are just going to end up being a "bother" to them in return.

Stephen's Definitions

Anger — Just one letter short of danger.

Self-Control — Something that comes in mighty handy when you're eating salted peanuts.

Temperance — A trait learned from a tea kettle—though it's up to it's neck in hot water, it continues to sing.

Peace — The period of confusion and unrest between two wars.

Patience — The art of concealing your impatience.

Cooperation — Doing what I tell you and doing it quickly.

GRACE'S SECTION

How to Heal Headaches and Pains in the Neck

For a headache you can take medicine. But what if your brother is the headache and he's bothering you like a mosquito? You can't flatten him with a flyswatter. If he's being a pain in the neck, a chiropractor can't fix him. Maybe the real thing that needs to be fixed is you!

Why do we get irritated? Think about it. I think it's because we're selfish. If we didn't care what happened to us or our stuff, we wouldn't get irritated! So when you are right in the middle of "being irritated" and you want to respond in the correct way, what do you do? Here are some ideas: 1) Ask God for help! 2) Pray for the one irritating you. 3) Quote Scripture to yourself. I like the verse Stephen mentioned in the end of his section. *"Be not overcome of evil, but overcome evil with good."* (Rom. 12:21)

We also need to make sure that we are not the ones doing the irritating. Sometimes it seems kind of fun to annoy our brothers and sisters, but then when they start annoying us it seems like torture! It helps to remember what Jesus said, *"All things whatsoever ye would that men should do to you, do ye even so to them."* (Matt. 7:12)

Mice Aren't Always Nice

A man at our church was trying to get rid of all the mice in his garage, so he set a trap. This trap was designed so that the mice would go after the cheese and fall in, one mouse at a time. The day after he set the trap, he went to look and see how many mice he had caught. He was in for a surprise. There were many mice, but only one mouse was still alive. When all those mice were confined to such small quarters, they would fight and fight until all but one was dead. This same thing happened every time the man set his mousetrap. Just like those mice, brothers and sisters spend a lot of time together and it's very easy to fight and be annoyed with each other. I am hoping this chapter will help you so that your family will not be like the mice in the box.

I've noticed that people act the way they are treated. If you treat your brother like he's a pain in the neck, don't be surprised if he starts acting like one! My dad says that if you treat people like you respect them, they will act respectable. If you take their side, they will be loyal to you. If you treasure them, they will be a treasure. Treat people the way you want them to act.

I'M PERPLEXED...

Question: Is there any way I can "change" my siblings, or do I have to just put up with them?

Answer: Everyone has flaws. It is easier to see other people's faults than our own. You may have perfectly good motives for wanting to "change" your brothers and sisters. Your goal may only be to help them to grow in the Lord and to make right decisions in their life. That is good, but you must still proceed with caution when trying to share their faults with them. Establish a good relationship with them first. Many times you will find that they will work on their weaknesses after you have worked on yours (remember the key from chapter six).

It is only after you have won their heart by your kindness and sensitivity, that they will be able to accept advice and suggestions from you. Even when you feel the freedom to do this, remember that praise is much more effective than criticism.

HIS Story Applied Today

How Come One Person Has to Do All the Work?

What kind of things irritate you most about your siblings? Have you ever noticed their lack of character traits and wished you could point these out to them?

A certain lady named Martha felt that way. Her sister, Mary, was not acting or helping in the way that Martha thought she should. Most days it would probably have been okay, but not this day! It was a super busy day and there was so much to do. The meals needed to be prepared, the house needed to be cleaned, and the company needed to be cared for. By the way, it wasn't just any company, it was *Jesus, Himself.* Martha was running here and there, wondering how in the world she was going to get everything done. And to top it all off, she was frustrated with Mary. Even though Martha was frantically serving and felt under pressure, Mary was just sitting around. In fact, Mary didn't even seem to notice the work—she was oblivious to it all, sitting at Jesus' feet.

Finally, Martha could take it no longer. She came to Jesus and said, *"Lord, dost thou not care that my sister hath left me to serve alone? Bid her [Mary], therefore, that she help me."* (Luke 10:40) Jesus' response was not what Martha was expecting, for He replied, *"Martha, Martha, thou art careful and troubled about many things: But one thing is needful: and Mary hath chosen that good part, which shall not be taken away from her."* (Luke 10:41-42)

Let us be careful not to have a "Martha" attitude. She saw flaws in her sister and tried to correct them herself. Actually, Martha just wanted her sister to comply with her own priorities. Even if we do see character deficiencies in the lives of our siblings, it is not our place to change them. For in the end, Martha found out that her sister had actually chosen the better thing!

MASTER, TELL HER TO HELP. A LOT OF PEOPLE ARE GOING TO BE HERE TODAY. THERE'S A TON OF WORK TO DO. WHY SHOULD I HAVE TO DO IT ALL? SHE'S JUST SITTING AROUND DOING NOTHING BUT LISTENING TO YOU. LOOK AT ALL THE FOOD TO GET READY. IT'S TOO MUCH FOR ONE PERSON.

Self-Evaluation Quiz 7

1. When my brother irritates me...
- ❑ I keep track of everything he does so I can laugh about it with my friend.
- ☒ I begin to feel like a red hot.
- ❑ I hurry to the library to check out books on practical jokes.
- ☒ I am frustrated, confused, upset, and don't know what to do.
- ❑ I remember that this is all part of God's Training Program.

2. My verbal response to my sister's irritation is usually...
- ☒ "Leave me alone."
- ☒ "Get out of my room! Out! O-U-T spells OUT!"
- ❑ "MOM!"
- ❑ Silence.
- ❑ A soft answer, to turn away wrath.

3. When my brother asks, "Want to know what I did today?" I feel...
- ☒ Suddenly busy.
- ❑ Bored.
- ❑ Disturbed.
- ☒ Glad.
- ❑ Aggravated.

4. When I am sitting at a restaurant and my little brother kicks me under the table, the best response is to...
- ❑ Begin a conversation about soccer.
- ❑ Kick the person to my right and say, "Pass it on!"
- ❑ Yell, "OUCH!" and then glare at my brother for at least a minute.
- ❑ Ask for shin guards when the waitress comes to our table.
- ❑ Fill out a nasty response form for the restaurant telling about my uncomfortable meal.
- ❑ Ignore it until the proper time to discuss it with my brother.
- ❑ Repay evil with good.

CHAPTER EIGHT

The Door to My Room is Locked

Three Life-Changing Attitudes

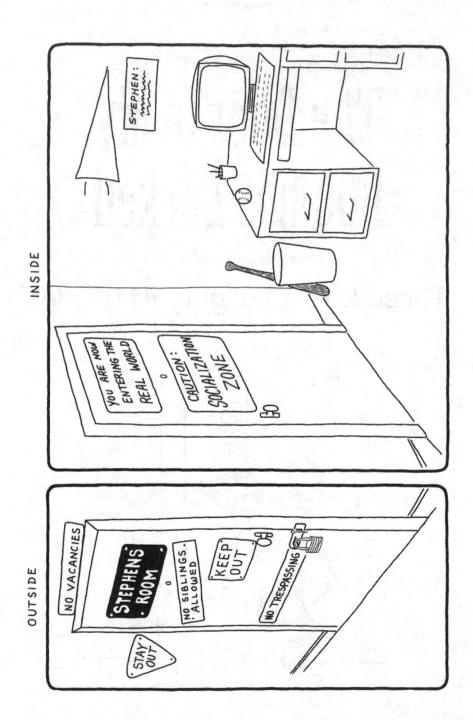

SARAH'S SECTION

Three Life-Changing Attitudes

You can walk into any bookstore and find all sorts of books that will give you formulas and solutions to solve all sorts of problems. But ultimately, we do not want to rely on formulas. Following a list of steps, as if we are following a recipe, is not the true answer. Though we need to have the right actions, they must stem from the right attitudes. The solution to conflicts is godliness—becoming like Christ.

To avoid allowing this chapter to be a book within a book, we have limited it to three of the most important attitudes in relationships. Our attitudes usually affect others even more than our actions do.

Sensitivity

Seeing beyond the surface to the real needs of those I am with

One time Jesus took a shortcut through a town that was not part of Israel. The people didn't like Israelites. They weren't friendly and wouldn't let Jesus and His disciples stay in their town. James and John got upset with this rude attitude and wanted to call down fire from heaven on the town.

But Jesus could see past the grouchy attitudes on the surface and He could tell what was really bothering the townspeople. They needed help—not punishment. He simply took His disciples to another town. But He rebuked James and John by saying, *"Ye know not what manner of spirit ye are of. For the Son of man is not come to destroy men's lives, but to save them."* (Luke 9:52-56)

When someone acts immaturely, instead of becoming upset, we should learn to identify some area of need in this person's life. Rather than reacting to the problem, we should be sensitive to any ways we could help their need.

- If he brags, it shows his need for humility and security.
- If he is angry, it shows his need for meekness and self-control.
- If he has bad friends, it shows his need for discernment.
- If he does wrong things, it shows his need for the fear of the Lord.
- If he's not friendly, it shows his need for hospitality and kindness.
- If he's wasteful, it shows his need for resourcefulness.

Sensitivity in Our Family

I could tell you many stories of times in my life when I have been encouraged because Stephen and Grace were sensitive to my needs. Grace is able to sense when I am sad or discouraged and she looks for ways to encourage me. Stephen is able to see needs right away; he often takes care of problems before others even notice them. When I'm involved in a project, he is always helping with behind-the-scenes work that I forgot about. He is sensitive to my needs and available to help with them. This is a tremendous blessing in my life and ministry.

In chapter four, Grace told a story about how she hid behind a bush because she was upset about something Stephen, Mom, and I had said. One interesting aspect of that story is that the three of us did not even know anything was wrong. We had not been sensitive. When it was time to leave, no one could find Grace. Dad finally found her hiding behind a bush. She seemed upset and didn't want to get in the car. No one had any idea why. Once we figured out what the problem was, I felt convicted; I had not even realized that we had bothered Grace. I just thought it was funny and I had no idea that it had hurt her. Thus, my lack of sensitivity caused an unnecessary problem.

Even though we live with our brothers and sisters, we may not really know them as well as we think we do. If we do not take the time to listen to them, see their needs, and understand them, we may just be living our own lives, oblivious to how they need our support and encouragement. You may be surprised about how many things there are in your siblings' lives that you are not aware of ...

The Things that Go On Behind Closed Doors

It used to be that when Grace took a bath, she'd take a LONG time. That's because she did more than take a bath—the whole Rubber Ducky National Racing Tournament took place while she was in there ...

... On numerous occasions, one of us would be walking by the bathroom and hear the commotion. He or she would quietly gather the rest of the family, and we'd all stand around with our ear to the bathroom door to join in on the excitement. (Of course, we'd be sure to be perfectly quiet, so as not to disturb. Hopefully, the muffled laughing didn't bother the duckies.) We would hear something like this:

"The race is now beginning. Fluffy takes the lead, but Puffy is close behind. Go, Puffy! Go, Quacky! Oh, what's this? Squeaky is catching up. Squeaky takes the lead! Puffy just turned over. I think he's having a hard time. Come on, Quacky! Squeaky is far ahead. Oh, I think we have a winner. It's Squeaky! Congratulations! And the crowd cheers."

Who knows? There may be adventures, exciting events, and interesting circumstances occurring in the lives of your brother and sister that you do not know about. Your siblings may be making important decisions. Meaningful things are happening in their lives. In Grace's section of this chapter, she explains practical ways to show sensitivity to what is behind the door. Each of us has aspects of our lives that are behind closed doors. We may be missing a lot more than we know, due to our lack of sensitivity.

Meekness

Giving up my rights and dying to my wants, knowing that God is actually in charge

John 12:24 says, *"Verily, verily, I say unto you, Except a corn of wheat fall into the ground and die, it abideth alone; but if it die it bringeth forth much fruit."*

Recently, Grace and I were making a cake for my mom's birthday. I thought it should be round, but Grace thought it should be square. I bought a cheap cake mix, but she thought I should have bought an expensive one. I thought it should have chocolate frosting, but she was sure that white frosting would be better. She wanted to decorate it with flowers and green leaves, but I thought that would be too much work. I wanted to get it done quickly, but she wanted to take the time to do it right and make it fancy. Needless to say, the two of us were not seeing eye to eye on our little project. What should we do?

The answer is that we needed to understand and apply meekness. Meekness is not merely giving up **things**, but more importantly, it is giving up our **position**, or the privileges of our position. When the older one gives up his privileges as oldest—that's meekness. Also, meekness is giving up one's need to win—especially in a discussion. This is why meekness made it to the "Big Three." Nothing stops arguments faster than meekness. That's what meekness is—the ability to not argue because you recognize there is **nothing** to win, but much to lose. Meekness is being able to say, "Good point. You might be right, I'll think about that," and "I thought this was a good idea, but yours is good, too." Since arguments are one of the biggest problems between siblings, the skill of avoiding them is a key element.

What Makes Meekness Hard?

- It is voluntarily putting yourself underneath another.
- It is submitting to someone even though they may not officially have authority over you.

What Makes Meekness Easy?

- It is feeling no need to fight with "employees" because you are personal friends with the "Boss" (our Heavenly Father).
- It is understanding that there is no need to worry about the outcome of a certain matter, because you know that God is in charge and you always enjoy His surprises.

One day, when I was about fifteen years old, our family arrived at my grandma's house for a visit. We were planning to stay at her house for several days, so the first job was to move in and unpack. Her house is very small and crowded, as you may remember from Stephen's story in the last chapter. Every time we stayed with her, Stephen and Grace would sleep in the living room with Grandma and I would sleep in a small bed in the bedroom. As we were unpacking, Mom came to me and said, "You have been sleeping in the bedroom every time we come. It is Stephen's turn now."

My first thought was, "Wait a minute! That's my only space of privacy in this house. How am I going to get any work done in the living room?" Then I remembered that I had recently learned some things about meekness. A meek person doesn't fight for their rights. Instead, they give all their rights to the Lord and trust Him to take care of everything. I decided not to complain about my problem to Mom or Stephen, but just to pray that the Lord would work out the right person to sleep there. Guess what? A few minutes later, Stephen came up to me and said, "I know you'd like to sleep in that bed, and that's fine with me. I will sleep in the living room." If you demonstrate meekness, you will find that God often abundantly provides for you in unexpected ways.

You will find more insights on meekness when you read Stephen's section of this chapter.

Compassion

Gently healing hurts because we are able to feel how others have been wrongfully injured

Sensitivity is seeing the need; compassion is feeling for the need and doing something about it. The gospels mention nine specific times that

Jesus showed compassion—that is more than any other quality. Mark 6:34 says, *"And Jesus, when He came out, saw much people, and was moved with compassion toward them, because they were as sheep not having a shepherd: and He began to teach them many things."*

There are many things that a person will automatically do right if he has compassion, and automatically do wrong if he does not have compassion. Therefore, compassion is the foundation for many other responses. Here are some keys to remember:

- True compassion will give over and over again. (Lam. 3:22-23)
- Compassion is NOT based upon what another deserves; after all, none of us deserve the Lord's compassion for us.
- Compassion is suffering inwardly for someone else who is suffering outwardly.

When I see someone suffer it is easy for me to think, "He is getting what he deserves because of his wrong decisions." Jesus could have said that, too, but He didn't. He looked upon the people as helpless and sacrificially gave to them and helped them. I have learned compassion by watching my parents, and the way they have treated us when we were sad or in need.

This is silly, I remember thinking. *Dad and Mom are not going to like Grace waking them up over such a little thing.*

Our family was staying overnight in a cabin at a Christian camp. In the room where Grace and I were sleeping, there were bunk beds that were stacked three high. Grace (who was eight) was really excited as she chose the bunk bed she wanted to sleep on.

"I've never slept on a bunk bed this high before," she said enthusiastically. "This is going to be fun."

We climbed into bed and turned off the lights. After a few minutes I heard a soft voice:

"Sarah," Grace said timidly, "This bunk bed is really high. What if I roll off during the night? Do you think it might be dangerous?"

"Well, Grace," I replied, "If you're worried about it, why don't you just move down to a lower bunk."

Grace thought for a minute and then answered, "But Sarah, this is the *only* time that we'll ever be staying at this camp. And I really like this bunk. This is my *only* chance to ever sleep on it!"

"Oh, well if it means that much to you—just stay there," I said. "I'm sure you'll be fine."

I shut my eyes and tried to sleep. But a few minutes later, I heard …

… "Sarah," do you think maybe I *should* move down to that lower bunk?"

"If you're still thinking about it, Grace, then just switch bunks. The lower ones will feel the same as the one you're on now."

"But, Sarah, this is the only time we'll be at this camp, and this is my only chance—"

"Grace, I'm sure you'll be fine," I repeated, "Don't worry about it. You won't roll off. Just go to sleep."

Once again, I shut my eyes. But soon I heard a familiar voice.

"Sarah, I just don't know what I should do."

Then Grace started to cry. Finally, she decided to go ask Mom and Dad about her situation. She left me lying in bed, wondering how my parents would like being awakened over such a little problem.

A few minutes later I heard Dad coming into the room with Grace. Instead of being annoyed, he was looking at the situation from Grace's perspective. He said, "So, you'd really like to sleep on this bunk bed? Well, let's see what we can figure out."

Then using a suitcase and bracing it securely in place, he built a little wall so that she would be able to sleep in the top bunk without being scared. Grace went to bed happy, and both Grace and I remembered my dad's example of compassion. It may have been inconvenient for my dad that night, but it sure meant a lot to Grace!

Where Should I Sit?

Everyday we have the opportunity to demonstrate compassion if we choose to invest in the lives of other people. Recently, I was at a dinner with a group of families. After going through the line, I headed toward a table where some of my friends were sitting. As I walked to this table, anxious to talk to my friends, I passed a girl sitting by herself and I invited her to come sit with us. She said she didn't want to, so I just passed on by. Then I changed my mind and decided to go sit with her. During lunch, she began to open up to me and we had a nice talk. I didn't think very much of the incident until her parents came up to me afterwards. They both expressed how thankful they were that I talked to her. They explained that she was going through a hard time, but didn't want to talk with them about it. They were thrilled when they saw her talking with me. This story reminded me that showing sensitivity and compassion is often inconvenient. God has opportunities for us to demonstrate Christ-like love everyday. If we are not attentive, it is easy to miss these opportunities.

Your Chance to Apply This May Be Just Around the Corner

Last night, I was typing on the computer, working on this book. I was deep in concentration and was trying to avoid all distractions.

Just then Grace walked up to me and was eager to tell me about her day. I listened to her patiently, but responded with a simple, "That's nice," anxious to get back to my work. Just as I got my mind back on my sentence, Grace called to me from around the corner, "Sarah, I didn't know you still had that little tent in your closet. Did you know that it's still there?"

"Yes," I responded and continued typing. (No, I wasn't writing the chapter on irritations.)

"Why?" she called out again.

"Because I still want it," I said in the shortest number of words possible, hoping I did not sound irritated.

After about eight seconds of silence, she said, "Is it hard to set up, Sarah?"

Before I had a chance to answer, I heard Mom call to Grace from the living room, "Could you be a little quieter, honey? I'm trying to concentrate."

(I thought to myself, "ME, TOO! Thanks, Mom!")

"Oh—sorry," Grace said.

I had several blissful minutes without interruptions. Wow! Perhaps this would be a record. Then I noticed a strange white stick floating around in the air, right above the keyboard. I recognized it as a tent pole. I ignored it and continued typing, but then a new thought came to me: Grace is just trying to have fun. She assumes that it is the end of the day and time for a break. She wants me to play along with her game ... so, instead of ignoring her, I said, "Look at this! A tent pole!" and I pulled off the end of it.

Grace smiled and said, "Put that back on. I'm going to go scare Stephen with this tent pole now."

"Great idea!" I thought. "Good-bye!"

Everyday, almost every minute, we can be demonstrating these three traits of godliness. As sensitivity, meekness, and compassion become a pattern in our lives, we will see unexpected benefits in our relationships with our siblings. We may never know just how much we have impacted their lives.

A Three-Year-Old's Laws:

- If I like it, it's mine.
- If it's in my hand, it's mine.
- If I can take it from you, it's mine.
- If I had it a little while ago, it's mine.
- If it's mine, it must never appear to be yours in any way.
- If I'm doing or building something, all the pieces are mine.
- If it looks just like mine, it is mine.
- If I saw it first, it's mine.
- If you are playing with something and you put it down, it automatically becomes mine.
- If it's broken, it's yours!

                    - Developed by James Quinn

Our Own Laws:

- Don't use my things without asking.
- If you borrow my things, I expect to have them returned to me in the same condition in which I gave them to you.
- I have the right to decide how I want to use my time.
- I have the right to work on my own projects without being bothered.
- I have the right to make my own decisions.
- I have the right to my own space.

God's Laws

- Everything belongs to the Lord. (Ps. 24:1)
- Anything we have, including our own bodies, belongs to God. (I Cor. 6:20)
- We are only stewards of the things God has given us. (Mt. 25:20-21)
- It is God's responsibility to protect His own property. (Rom. 12:19)
- We have no rights at all. (Gal. 2:20)
- Rather than standing up for our wants, we must die to ourselves. (Jn. 12:24-25)

TEASING: DANGER ZONE

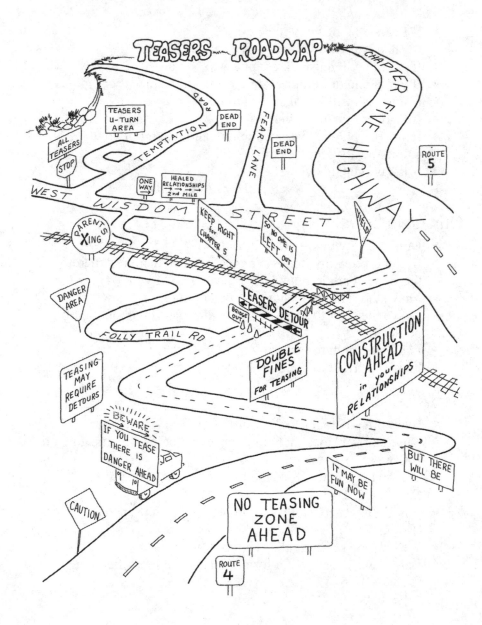

STEPHEN'S SECTION

Clash Collision Episode

This is Reporter Mailbox for WABC, with a newsflash from the backyard. It's a nice, bright, sunny day and about 82° F. There's a slight breeze coming from the south and not a cloud in the sky. Thank you for joining us for the Clash Collision episode. Little Johnny looks out the window and sees the tire swing with nobody on it. He cannot resist the urge to dash out there and become a part of this beautiful scene. Then he sees a terrible sight. His brother, Phillip, is already in the front yard and walking towards the tire swing. He makes a quick decision to dash for it, determined to arrive there before his brother. He races out the front door, makes a wide turn, and aims directly for the swing. Then his brother, Phillip, sees this blur tearing across the lawn. He realizes that he is going to have to speed up to make it to the swing before his brother does. And they're off. Thirty feet separate them. Now twenty. Now ten. Now five. Smash! Crunch! Bang! Our two blurs just made a crash landing on the swing. Johnny grabs the swing and Phillip grabs Johnny. They both start pulling, and now the picture perfect lawn on the bright, sunny day has turned into a war zone.

Why? It's simple. Both Johnny and Phillip were fighting for their wants. There was something they wanted, and they were determined to get it. Our wants often get us into trouble. It may not be a tire swing—it may be the front seat of the car, the shower in the morning, or time on the computer. Whatever it is, I can guarantee you that things would go a lot smoother if we were willing to give up our wants. "That's ridiculous!" you yell. But you are mistaken, it is not ridiculous. It's meekness!

How can I be meek? Good question. I have a good answer. All those things you think are yours (toys, time, reputation, sleep, three good meals a day, etc.) are not really yours at all. Everything belongs to God. (Ps. 24:1) Why do you get mad when someone hurts your things, wastes your time, or eats your lunch? You say, "I get upset because it's mine! That belongs to me." Stop right there. Don't say anymore. It's not yours—it's God's. If God allows someone else to swing on His tire swing, why are you angry about it? It's not yours in the first place. Meekness is being willing to lose things, time, money, comfort, advantage, reputation, praise, position of leadership, and status in the eyes and minds of others. When we have nothing to lose (because it's not ours, it's God's), we have no reason to ever get angry. If you can apply this one thing, you will have the key to overcoming anger.

Lose to Gain

A meek person understands that God is the One who will give him his reward. When Sarah has a Bright Lights conference going on, I usually have to pick up all of the odds and ends. I end up making copies, hole punching, cutting and sorting papers, running sound, video taping, and remembering other things that have to be done. So after the conference is over, a lot of people will tell the Bright Lights Leaders how good it was. But what about me? Nothing. Silence. I am just the person in the background. But when we are trying to be meek, we can't ask for recognition. We have to remember who we are really working for: God. And God sees all of the work we do. *"Well done thou good and faithful servant."* (Matt. 25:21) Notice it says servant—a servant is someone

who works behind the scenes. (I might add that after the conference Sarah is very appreciative to the rest of our family.)

So, when you are about to have a crash collision at your house, pause, and forfeit your wants. Choose to give in to others, instead of forcing your own way. It is far better to be the winner in God's eyes than the winner in men's eyes.

Stephen's Definitions

Charity — Something that should begin at home, but most people don't stay at home long enough to begin it.

Character — Have it. Don't be one.

Mistake — The first one usually made is opening your mouth.

Conscience – It may be a still, quiet voice, but it sure yells loudly afterwards.

Diplomacy — The art of letting someone else get your way.

GRACE'S SECTION

Applying Sensitivity

I was discouraged one day because I had a lot of schoolwork to do and I felt like I wasn't getting anything done. I was upset and my day just wasn't going well. Stephen put a letter on my desk. It said something like this:

> *Dear Grace,*
> *You are doing great on school! Keep working! If you get it all done, we can play!*
> *Love, Stephen*

Stephen used the computer to print it out with a picture. Although this happened several years ago, I still remember it. It was simple and short, but it really encouraged me! You show sensitivity when you see a need and do something about it. Stephen recognized my need when my school wasn't going well, and he took action to help my day go better.

Imagine that there is a container of strawberries sitting on the table. As you walk by, you naturally pick the biggest, ripest, juiciest one, right? Human beings tend to care only about themselves. But the Bible says, *"Thou shalt love thy neighbor as thyself."* (Matt. 22:39) To show sensitivity means to care about your brother and sister, and think about what will benefit them, instead of just caring about yourself.

You Can't Do Anything if You Don't Notice!

You might think that "noticing" is a small and easy part of sensitivity, but that's not true. Sometimes when my feelings are hurt, it just seems like Sarah and Stephen don't notice. They aren't trying to be insensitive—they just don't notice! Sometimes we are upset and we just want someone to talk to us and encourage us, but no one even recognizes that anything is wrong. Since we know what this feels like, it should motivate us to show sensitivity to our brothers and sisters when they need encouragement. These questions may help you determine when your brother or sister is feeling bad.

- Is he being unusually quiet?
- Does he seem lost in another world?

- When you ask him a question, does he hear you? Does he answer?
- Does he avoid answering the telephone?
- Is he slouching or stomping around?
- Is he acting unusual by not whistling or singing around the house?
- Is he often in his room with the door shut?
- Is he acting tired and lazy?
- Does he just disappear for a while?
- Is it the little problems that are really frustrating him?
- Is he more sensitive to teasing than he normally is?

Of course, the list will be a little different for each person. If you have trouble noticing, you could make a list of how your brothers and sisters act when they are upset—then you will be able to see their needs, even if they don't tell you about their struggles.

Now What Should I Do?

When your brother or sister is sad or upset, here are some ideas of ways to encourage them:

- Ask them what you can do for them.
- Write them a note.
- Pray for them and tell them that you are praying for them.
- Listen to them if they want to talk to you.
- Do something you know they like.
- Use Bible verses to encourage them.
- Praise them.
- Ask them what went wrong
- Encourage them by helping them to see things from God's perspective.
- Bring them a snack.
- Ask them how they are doing.
- Give them a gift—maybe a chocolate kiss!
- Make sure you are not the one causing the problem.

Special Notice for Families of Three or More:

Try to spend equal amounts of time with each of your brothers and sisters. Don't have too many "inside jokes" with just one sibling. Sometimes laughing a lot with only one sibling, or saying how you have a special thing in common with one will cause the other one to feel left out.

I'M PERPLEXED...

Question: But this is impossible; you don't know my brother!

Answer: You're right, I don't know your brother. I don't know you, either. Could he be saying the same thing about you?

God does know your brother and He has given him to you as a gift. Joseph's brothers were just about the worst—they sold him as a slave. Yet Joseph accepted it as part of God's plan. The more difficult the situation is, the more glory there will be for God when your relationship is healed. If this is totally impossible for you, you will be forced to depend on the Lord. Then you will have a testimony to share with others about God's power, and how God's ways work in even the hardest situations.

"Who comforteth us in all our tribulation, that we may be able to comfort them which are in any trouble, by the comfort wherewith we ourselves are comforted of God." (II Cor. 1:4)

HIS STORY APPLIED TODAY

They Don't Deserve Forgiveness

"If anyone had a right to be angry, it would have been me! If anyone had a right to punish my brothers, it would have been me! I've been suffering for years because of their cruelty. I've been miserable, hungry, mistreated, forgotten, despised, and tortured because of what they did. Now I finally have a chance to get back at them."

Can you imagine Joseph feeling this way? If he would have had this attitude, think of how all of history would have been affected. Let's jump back about twenty years in Joseph's life and see this from his brothers' perspective:

"It's not fair that our brother gets all the attention," they grumbled.

"Yeah, and Dad is always finding fault with us, but he's always praising Joseph."

"Did you hear about the gift Dad just gave him?"

"Dad never gives the rest of us anything."

"I can't take this anymore."

Joseph's brothers allowed their jealousy to increase and continue. Whenever you allow wrong thoughts of jealousy, they will lead to more problems. In Joseph's case, they finally sold him as a slave. They showed no compassion for his tears. They were not willing to give up their rights and show meekness. They showed the opposite of sensitivity and love, thinking only of themselves.

Joseph, on the other hand, is a perfect example of compassion and meekness. Not only did he forgive his brothers, he also provided for them, blessed them, and loved them. What gave Joseph the ability to have this attitude? Joseph was able to look at the situation from God's perspective. Through faith he understood that what his brothers meant for evil, God actually meant for good. This faith in God enabled him to treat his brothers in a godly way.

Although, hopefully, none of us are going to sell our brother as a slave, we must guard against the same attitude of jealousy that Joseph's brothers displayed. Have your parents ever praised your sibling, and you felt like you should have been praised, too? Do you ever feel like your brother gets more attention or that your parents like him better? If you struggle with thoughts of jealousy, choose to follow the example of Joseph and not of his brothers. His brothers allowed wrong thoughts to lead to bitterness and wrong actions. Joseph rejected wrong thoughts and chose to repay evil with forgiveness and compassion.

Self-Evaluation Quiz 8

How well do you know your brothers and sisters?

Would you be able to tell me the following things about your brothers and sisters?
- ❑ The last time they were sick?
- ❑ With what friends do they enjoy spending time?
- ❑ How they are feeling today?
- ❑ How they get along with your parents?
- ❑ What things hurt and irritate them the most?
- ❑ When their birthday is?
- ❑ What they like to do in their free time?
- ❑ When they became a Christian?
- ❑ Whether they prefer to stay up late or get up early?
- ❑ What books, people, or messages have influenced them the most?
- ❑ What their favorite kind of ice cream is?
- ❑ What struggles they are going through right now?
- ❑ Whether they prefer outside or inside chores?
- ❑ What their goals in life are?
- ❑ What upcoming event they are most excited about?

How Did You Do?

Evaluation: If you knew:

0   The first step for you is to make sure you know your brother/ sister's name.

1-3   You might want to have your vision and hearing tested.

4-6   Start taking surveys to make up for lost time.

7-9   You're doing pretty well, but don't be too confident. Try spending a little less time talking and more time listening.

10-12   You know plenty of information useful for bribes, threats, gift purchasing, and persuading. Better, this will help you understand the needs of your siblings and minister to them.

13-15   Congratulations! You should work for a detective service!

The GOOD Fight

(thoughts from our dad)

- The GOOD fight is not with flesh and blood but against a bigger enemy.
- The GOOD fight starts on our knees and in the Word.
- The GOOD fight is fought in our hearts and minds.
- The GOOD fight is often enjoyable to fight.
- The GOOD fight is against unseen enemies that the world is constantly defeated by.
- The GOOD fight is most often against ourselves and within ourselves.
- The GOOD fight is often won by losing.
- The GOOD fight is not against brothers and sisters but for them.
- The GOOD fight is hard but peaceful. A bad fight is easy but turbulent.
- The GOOD fight, if fought, is never ultimately lost.
- The GOOD fight is never an angry one.
- The GOOD fight transforms enemies into allies.
- The GOOD fight is won by surrender.
- The GOOD fight can't be won with arguments.
- The GOOD fight leads others to peace.
- The GOOD fight requires greater skill than a bad fight.
- The GOOD fight has many unseen victories. A bad fight leaves many unseen victims.

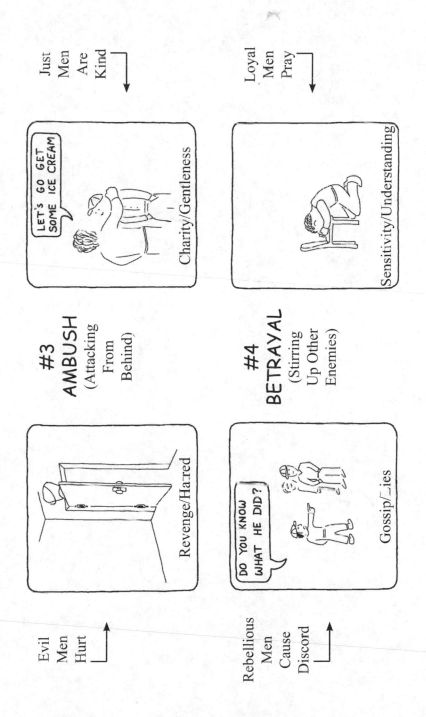

CHAPTER NINE

Too Big, Too Small, Too Short, Too Tall

What's Your Birth Order?

Sarah's Section

What's Your Birth Order?

Stephen is our computer expert. He really knows his stuff. Unfortunately, he also keeps seeing a need for additional, expensive equipment.

One day I was sitting in the living room when Stephen came in and said to me, "Sarah, for me, getting a laptop is kind of like you getting married."

This took me by surprise. "I wouldn't quite make that comparison," I said, "but what makes you say that?"

"Well," Stephen continued, "getting a laptop is something I've always looked forward to, and I won't be able to believe it if it actually happens."

So, I replied to him, "Hmm ... but Stephen, what about *you* getting married?"

He responded, "Sarah, that would be like you getting a laptop."

As anyone might expect, Stephen, Grace, and I are quite different. The same thing is true in every family; birth orders, personalities, and interests make every person in the world unique. Understanding these differences will help us relate properly to each other.

A Herald to Firstborns

I, being the oldest, have the job of writing to you firstborns. Have you noticed that being the firstborn can be difficult? You may feel that you have the most work, the most responsibility, and that others expect the most from you.

Being the oldest may seem like a problem at times, but actually, it is an asset. Not only do you have the biggest responsibility, you also have the most influence. If **you** are working towards better relationships, your family is headed toward success. Likewise, if you have problems with your siblings, you need to be willing to take the blame, and consider it your responsibility to improve things. You are the oldest, most mature, and in the place of greatest influence.

Remember the story of the prodigal son who left home with his share of the inheritance? (Luke 15:11-32) Why do you think the prodigal son left home in the first place? There are several reasons, but I think one reason is that he was rejected by his older brother. When he returned home, his older brother did not rejoice or welcome him—instead, he was jealous. If the older brother had been the right kind of brother all along, maybe the younger one would never have left home at all.

When I was about eleven years old, my mother took me out to breakfast. She wanted to explain to me how much influence I had on Stephen and Grace. She gave me a list of ways that I could encourage them.

Most firstborns do not realize the power they have. Our younger brothers and sisters notice us, look up to us, love attention from us, and copy us; they naturally want to please us. This puts us in a tremendous position to influence them. If we praise them for doing the right things, this is going to be an increased motivation for them to continue these things. Sometimes younger brothers and sisters are desperately trying to please us. They serve us, help us, and do things for us, but we simply take it for granted. They are all excited, expecting praise, but they get nothing at all (or even worse—criticism).

You might be thinking, "You are wrong. My younger brother or sister does not want to please me." If this is true, it is a sign of a bigger problem. I'll explain what I mean. Younger brothers and sisters naturally want to please the older ones. However, when offenses take place and they become hurt or bitter, this attitude can be reversed. Then instead of wanting to please you, they purposely **want** to displease and annoy you. You are now in a more difficult situation and must find the root problem (as discussed in chapters four through six). However, younger brothers and sisters usually really do want to please you, whether you know it or not.

Common Weaknesses of Firstborns:
- Bossing younger ones around or nagging them.
- Making all the decisions.
- Demanding or expecting too much.
- Constantly finding fault or criticizing.
- Being too busy for younger siblings.
- Overlooking the needs of the younger ones.
- Being embarrassed by them, rather than being proud of their unique features and strengths.
- Pushing our own ideas. (That's my specialty!)
- Leaving the younger ones out.
- Considering ourselves to be more important than they are.
- Being too controlling.
- Trying to change the faults we see in our siblings.

- Teasing and laughing for fun, without realizing the hurt we are causing.
- Taking advantage of younger siblings.

Because the firstborn is the oldest, and the one who is looked up to, it seems that he gets his way most of the time. Stop and think about your relationship with your brother or sister the last few days. Have you made the final decisions? Have you gotten your way? When Stephen and I were little, we played a lot of different things together (Legos, puppies, cars and trucks, house, etc.). Looking back, we find it amusing that I was always the one who decided what would happen and which toys we would use. As Grace grew older, she and Stephen spent a lot of time playing together. Then it was Stephen's turn to make all the decisions and control the game. Grace complains that she never got to play dolls or house—just cars and trucks, football, Legos, and tinker toys. Firstborns seem to often find ways to take advantage of the younger ones.

My mother is also a firstborn. One day when she was little, her mother gave her a candy bar to share with her younger brother. She said to my mother, "I want you to divide the candy bar and then let your brother choose first which piece he wants." My mother agreed, and carefully divided the bar into **three** pieces. Her brother chose one and she took the other two!

Important Considerations for Firstborns:

- Set a good example.
  After a few years of home schooling, the Lord convicted me that I was making things difficult for my mother by complaining about our household jobs. Later, I noticed that Stephen had picked up my bad attitude, and was also not cooperating with household jobs. I've found that Stephen and Grace often imitate my attitude. If I am cheerful, they are cheerful. If I complain, they complain. There have been many times that I have become annoyed with something about Stephen and Grace, only to realize that I was doing the same thing!
- Be willing to learn from them.
  Just because they are younger does not mean that they can't give you good ideas and insights.
- Express love.
  You can do this by acts of kindness, your tone of voice, your words, etc.
- Protect them from wrong influences, wrong friends, and wrong information.
- Include them in your life.
  When I go to the store, I love to have Stephen and Grace come along with me. It's always nice to have your best friends along, right? Stephen is usually the one who goes on errands with me. He is able to make a boring trip to the store a fun adventure. Funny things always seem to happen when Stephen is along. People who observe us often think that Stephen is my boyfriend. After all, why would a brother and sister want to be together?
- Pray for them daily.
- Don't have expectations.
  Accept them the way they are, rather than trying to get them to fit into your mold of what you think they should be like.
- Take initiative to do projects with them.

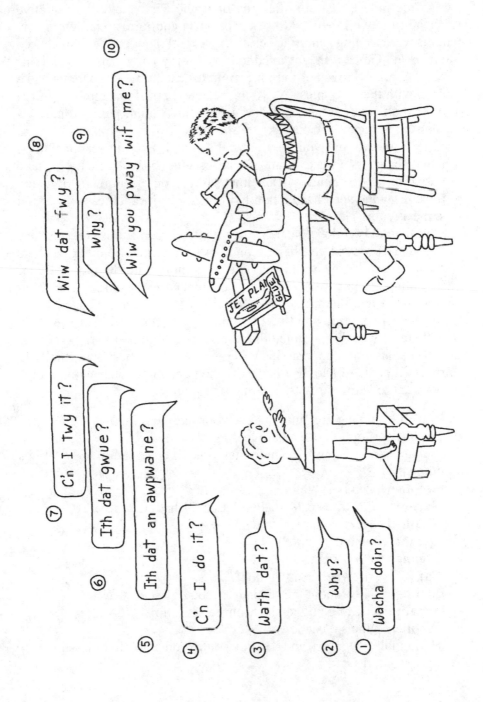

As the oldest, you are often the one who has to take the initiative to spend time with them or to begin projects and ministries. Once, my parents were leading a marriage class for several other couples, so I asked Stephen and Grace if they wanted to pray for my parents as they led this class. We prayed together for a few minutes each time my parents had a session with these couples. As young people, part of our ministry ought to be to make our parents' ministry successful. Often, family ministries never happen because no one takes the initiative to organize and start them. You have no excuse: you are the firstborn and it's your responsibility. If it will help, let's make it an official assignment! As firstborn, take initiative either to spend special time with a younger brother or sister, or to suggest and spearhead a family ministry project. (Please write and give me a report.)

I will quickly follow that up by saying that I realize this is not as easy as it sounds. Maybe you have found, as I have, that younger brothers and sisters are not always that anxious to comply with the ideas of their older sibling. When I was fourteen, I began playing the harp. After about six months, I had the great idea of teaching Stephen and Grace. I was so excited! I set up lesson times and practice sheets and began to work with them. I was disappointed that things didn't go as I was expecting. In fact, I soon found out that this was going to be the best opportunity to learn patience that I had ever had! Stephen and Grace insisted that they didn't want to learn to play the harp or the piano.

Sarah: Stephen, it's time to have your harp lesson.
Stephen: I don't need a harp lesson.
Sarah: Yes, you do. I want to make sure we get one in today. Let's do it now.
Stephen: I'm busy now.
Sarah: Well, when can we do it? Let's schedule a time.
Stephen: Next January.
Sarah: How about 1:00?
Stephen: No, I'm busy then.
Sarah: Well, when can you do it?
Stephen: How about the second Tuesday of next week?
Sarah: No, I'm going to ask Mom to set it up.
Stephen: She's busy now.
(Eventually Stephen and Grace would come to their lesson only because Mom insisted.)

The lesson would go something like this:

Grace: I'm tired.

Sarah: Me, too, but play your piece. Now, Grace, don't slouch like that. Sit up straight. No, I don't mean perfectly straight like a straight pin. Come on. Do it right.

Grace: I don't even know why I'm having a lesson. I haven't practiced.

Sarah: Well, let's start. Put your finger on the string. Now move your hand a little higher on the string. No, not way up at the top of the harp. Can you move your hand a little lower now? No, not all the way to the floor.

Grace: Can we do this lesson later?

Sarah: Grace, your harp is not your pillow. Now, Grace, how many times do I have to tell you that you can't read your book during your lesson?

Grace: Are we finished yet?

(I finally came up with an elaborate system of prizes and rewards, and was able to make some progress with them. They are now very good musicians, but it wasn't an easy road.)

The more you work together as a family, the more you will see how God has designed your family the way it is. Each different personality, skill, and interest put together makes a complete package. As your family grows closer, you'll be excited to observe and share how God has been working. One of the things that has caused Stephen, Grace, and me to be best friends is that we love to share our lives with one another. We are able to talk together about things we couldn't say to other friends. After a busy day, we all want to get together and tell about our experiences. Usually, everyone's talking at the same time.

One Evening in Particular ...

We had just had a long, busy and eventful day. Everyone had things to say, stories to tell, or opinions about this or that. We were sitting around in the living room and chatting away. Since we were all so tired, nobody felt like making the effort to get up and go to bed. And of course, the longer we talked, the more tired we became. It wasn't long before part of the family was talking, but other members of the family were closing their eyes and beginning to snore ... zzz ...

I remember when Grace was little. About mid-evening she'd get tired and fall asleep—somewhere. It could be anywhere, usually on the floor, under a table or chair, or wherever she'd been playing. (It didn't matter to her whether the floor was carpeted or not.) So when it came time to go to bed, we would have to get up, go find Grace, and carry her to bed. I don't know if she ever wondered how she got there.

... Well, this night, when we were all talking in the living room, it ended up being like Grace's typical bedtime. The only difference was that Grace wasn't the only one who fell asleep on the floor. She was first all right, but next was Stephen, then Dad, then Mom (she got the couch), and finally me. The whole family, one-by-one, drifted off to sleep, and no one was left to drag everyone else to bed. Anyway, when the sun came up the next morning, we woke up and wondered what we were all doing on the living room floor. We were all dressed and ready for family devotions!

In a nutshell, there is great reason for you, as firstborns, to be encouraged. Since younger brothers and sisters truly do look up to older ones, you have an extraordinarily high chance for success if you begin to invest in their lives. Will not God hold the oldest and most mature responsible? If there are problems in your relationship, do not pass the blame on to someone else—take it yourself. Evaluate your life. How have you hurt or neglected the littler ones? Choose now to do everything you can to love, treasure, encourage, and motivate them. Now, let's see what Stephen and Grace have to say about second and third-borns. I'm just as curious as you are!

STEPHEN'S SECTION

A New Meaning of "Middle Man"

Well, Sarah is writing to the oldest siblings, Grace to the youngest, and all the rest of you are stuck with me (whether you are 2nd or 20th). Also, for me, I'm the only boy—in between two girls! Is that like being marooned on an island surrounded by savages? In this chapter I'm going to share some of the benefits and difficulties about being in the middle.

I have observed a very strange phenomenon. Sometimes, the firstborn has an idea, and expects the second-born to do it. For example, there was the time Sarah mentioned how funny it would be if I dumped the rest of my ice water down Dad's shirt. He was driving and we were in the backseat. Don't laugh. It wasn't very funny when it actually happened. Then one time, Sarah wrote a skit for the two of us to do together. I was supposed to be a dog and she said I needed a big nose. In order to accomplish this, Sarah tied an empty toilet paper roll to my nose. Every time I see that wonderful picture in our photo album, I think about the joys of being a "second-born."

If you are born second or somewhere in the middle, you may find yourself constantly competing. There is someone who is always ahead of you, so you have a tendency to look up to him and respect him. One advantage to this is that we can observe the things they do wrong in various situations, and learn from them so that we do not make the same mistakes. In other words, they learn the hard way and we learn the easy way.

Second-borns sometimes get left out of things or overlooked. It seems like the firstborn gets all the attention for being the oldest (like three million baby pictures), the last-born gets all the attention for being the littlest, but the middle ones don't get any attention at all.

Another difficulty is that people often expect you, as a second-born, to be just like the firstborn. Since we're not just like the firstborn (thankfully!), many second-borns think they have to compete with the older in order to get approval.

Now, there is an interesting thing about being in the middle. It's that you not only look up to someone, but someone also looks up to you. You also, like the firstborn, are in a great position of influence. Your younger siblings will take whatever they can get in the line of compliments. Believe me—I know. If you just give them a couple of nice words, smile at them, or laugh at their joke, this will mean a lot to them. We know how it is to be on the receiving side with our older siblings, so we know what our younger siblings want from us. Let's be the same kind of older sibling that we want our older one to be to us.

I will now direct my attention to the male readers. I'm sure you would agree with me that sisters are interesting people. My sisters usually carry around a lot of stuff. (It must be a tendency of first and third-borns. No, actually I think it's a tendency of girls.) So, as the only boy, they think that I am some kind of personal wheelbarrow. That may be a problem, but problems also have benefits. Most guys today don't understand their responsibility to "the weaker vessel." Guys are bigger and stronger than girls, and therefore, they should count it a privilege to protect them, help them with things they can't do, and show them special honor, respect, and courtesy. We should be polite and do the obvious things that are often overlooked, like putting gas in the car, and helping them carry things. (Just make sure they pay for the gas!) Try opening a door for your sister and see how she likes it.

Stephen's Definitions

Cheerfulness — It may be contagious, but it seems like some people have been vaccinated against the infection.

Chores — What to say you're doing if you want a few minutes by yourself.

Etc. — The perfect word when you can't think of the right one.

Impatience — Waiting in a hurry.

Firstborn's philosophy — Never put off till tomorrow what you can order someone else to do today.

Golden Rule — Something that may be old, but hasn't been used enough to show any signs of wear.

Energy — Something little brothers and sisters save for rainy days.

Females — People who take their time taking your time.

GRACE'S SECTION

Last But Not Least

Many times Sarah has spoken to others about how to get along with little brothers and sisters. Obviously, I don't have younger brothers or sisters and so her insights didn't really apply to me. I didn't think or worry about it. I just assumed it was *Sarah and Stephen's* responsibility to try to get along with ME!

Well, I have news for all the youngest ones. We have part of the responsibility, too. We have the choice of whether we want to be a "pest" or a "blessing." Do we want to make it hard or easy for our brothers and sisters?

We all want attention and approval from our big brothers and sisters. If we can't get attention by being nice or helpful, sometimes we go to the other extreme and try to get attention by being annoying. This makes it hard for everybody—including our parents. Is this what we want? I have experience in both, so I hope this list encourages you to be a blessing, instead of a pest.

How to Be a Blessing:

- Take them a snack while they are working.
- Be happy when they succeed; don't be jealous of them.
- Send little paper airplanes with notes on them into their room.
- Be helpful and cooperative when they baby-sit.
- Put away their bike for them.
- Tell your parents the good things you notice about them.
- Bring them flowers for their room. (To brothers maybe blue flowers? Or a toad. Well, that might not be a blessing to mom!)
- Surprise them by doing one of their chores secretly for them.
- Let them have the front seat of the car.
- Give them exceptional service when they are sick by making them cards, and taking them books, blankets, and things to do.
- Don't bother them when they want to be alone.
- When you first see your brother or sister in the morning, smile and cheerfully say, "Good morning! How did you sleep?"
- Surprise them with little candies on their dresser.
- Comply with what they want to do. In our family it is Sarah who comes up with the big "earth shaking" plans (like writing a BOOK!) So I have to decide whether I want to go along with her

or not. I've found that a big help in things like this is to see it from her perspective. How would I like it if I came up with this great idea, and then Sarah and Stephen didn't want to do it?

- Let them have the last serving of mashed potatoes at supper.
- Obey them. We younger ones don't like it when our older brother or sister tells us what to do, especially if they are not very much older then we are. But even if it goes against our pride, it is good practice for us to be humble and honor them.

How to Be a Pest:

If we let ourselves, we can be annoying, irritating, little pests, can't we? I'm sure our older siblings would agree this is quite a talent that we have!

- Constantly ask, "What are you doing?"
- Then, never fail to follow it up with a second question, "Why?"
- If they don't answer (or even if they do), this is a sure sign that you should ask the same question again, louder.
- Borrow their things. Make sure you scratch them or break them.
- See how long you can talk without stopping (except to take breaths).
- Go in their room and move things around.
- When their friends come over, this is the best time to show all your latest toys, tricks, pictures, or tell all your stories.
- Drink all the milk so they won't have any for breakfast.
- Always point out when they get details wrong in a story they are telling.
- Surprise them with all your junk on their bed.
- Always talk loudly. In fact, if you yell instead of talk, this really gets 'em.
- Get to the bathroom just before they do. Stay in there a long time.
- Go into their room early in the morning, flip the lights on, rip the covers off, and loudly exclaim, "It's time to get up!"
- Pound on their bedroom door every five minutes with something else to tell them.
- Bug them when they are trying to read an interesting book.
- Get a big smile on your face when they tell you that you are extremely annoying.
- When they ask you to pass the butter, leisurely spread the butter on your bread first.

- Tell them how thankful you are that you don't look like them.
- Tell them that you think their jokes are dumb.
- Always jump out from corners when they are not expecting it and scare them. (This is one of my specialties!)

HIS STORY APPLIED TODAY

Leave Me Alone, Little Brother!

This example in Scripture is just one of many stories that gives insights about how younger and older siblings relate. Some of you may never have heard of Eliab, but I expect that all of you have heard of his younger brother. Eliab was a handsome and tall young man. He was in the camp with the Israelites, fighting against the Philistines. One day Eliab's little brother showed up in the camp. He had been sent by his dad to bring gifts and find out how things were going.

Actually, things were not going very well at all. A giant named Goliath was mocking and defying the Israelites, but no one had the courage to fight him. All the Israelites were terrified. Eliab's little brother, whose name was David, couldn't believe this was happening. He began to ask questions, and wondered what would be given to the man who killed the giant.

Eliab became angry and said to David, "Why are you here? Who did you leave those few sheep with? I know your pride and wickedness. You just came here because you wanted to see the battle." (See I Samuel 17:28) Why did Eliab react this way to David? It seems like an unfair reaction. We all know the rest of the story. David refused to let the name of God be mocked by Goliath in this way. He fought the giant, even though everyone else in the Israelite army was afraid to. The Lord won a tremendous victory through David's faith.

So why was Eliab annoyed and irritated by David? It's because even though Eliab stood out as a leader in Israel (I Sam. 16:6), he wasn't fighting the giant as he should have been. Because of fear, he was not willing. Yet he did not want his little brother to show him up. I think it probably made Eliab feel guilty when David mentioned fighting the giant. It was Eliab's own guilt that caused him to be angry with his little brother, David. Eliab knew that he wasn't being the leader he should be.

I'M PERPLEXED...

Question: Is it ever okay to be a tattletale?

Answer: It all depends on your motive. If the reason you want to tell on your brother or sister is for your own good, or to get back at them, then, no, it is not okay. It will only cause your sibling to get upset with you, and will end up hurting your relationship, instead of helping it. Matthew eighteen tells us that when a brother offends us we should go and talk to them privately.

However, it is always a good idea to communicate with your parents, and to let them know your struggles. It is important to tell them everything and not to have any secrets from them. It's not wrong to share with your parents a need you see in the life of one of your brothers and sisters. But before you do this, examine your motives, and be sure that your goal is only for the good of your brother or sister. They need to know that you are for them—not against them.

Self-Evaluation Quiz 9

1. I show sensitivity to my brother/sister by...
☒ Sensing when they are angry and staying away.
☐ Noticing when they disobey and telling Mom.
☒ Remembering their birthday.
☒ Not reading their diary.
☐ Comforting them when they are sad.
☐ Learning what things hurt their feelings and avoiding them.
☒ Squirting the ketchup bottle at my food and not at them.

2. Other people think my brother/sister and I...
☒ Actually like each other.
☐ Are a hopeless situation.
☐ Are great wrestlers.
☒ Are sweet and perfect companions.
☒ Are a hilarious combination.
☐ Are in the middle of the Civil War.

3. I am willing to take the time just to listen to the concerns of my brother/sister...
☐ While I tie my shoe.
☐ When I'm asleep.
☒ If they listen to me.
☐ Do they have concerns?

4. When my sister is mean to me and offends me...
☐ I wish she would be like my dog. He asks no questions and gives no criticism.
☐ I realize this is a test from God.
☐ I decide that my enemies are less trouble than my family.
☒ I don't say anything, but I have a hard time forgiving her.

5. When my sister and I both want to use the computer at the same time, the best response is...

❑ To get behind the computer chair, push, and give her an exciting ride.

☒ To put up a sign on the computer which says, "By Reservation Only."

☒ To give up my rights.

❑ To pull the plug.

❑ To tell her that the computer is contagious and she might catch a virus.

6. When my sister wants to show me her loose tooth, I feel...

☒ Disgusted.

☒ Pleased.

❑ Honored.

❑ Surprised.

❑ Like the tooth fairy.

❑ That I have an opportunity to make her feel special.

❑ Faint.

7. My brother/sister thinks I...

☒ Am their full-time playmate.

❑ Don't exist.

❑ Enjoy playing follow-the-leader 24 hours a day.

☒ Have nothing to do but help them.

☒ Am a friend in whom they can confide.

❑ Am planning to write their autobiography.

CHAPTER TEN

Family Warfare

The Amazing Weapon Called Praise

SARAH'S SECTION

The Amazing Weapon Called "Praise"

Excitement beamed on the face of a little boy whose big brother was soon coming home from a camping trip. Even though he spent the morning diligently preparing for his brother's return, the time still seemed to go by very slowly as he waited. He put a "welcome home" sign on the door and asked his mom to make his brother's favorite cookies. These he set on the table right next to the nice, cold glasses of milk he had prepared. All was ready, and the little boy was waiting with eager anticipation.

At last, the door opened and in walked his big brother. The little boy's face brightened and he waited to see his brother's reaction. The older brother, however, didn't seem to notice any of these things, but walked with his friend toward his bedroom.

His little brother went running after him saying, "We made some cookies for you. Come and eat them with me!"

"I'm not hungry," the older brother said, as he entered his room with his friend and shut the door. The little brother's face fell and he slowly walked away.

Can you envision how this story could have had a much different ending if the older brother had been sensitive to his younger brother? Suppose the older brother had looked at the younger one with a radiant smile and said, "It's so good to see you. I've missed you. Wow! Look at these cookies. Thank you for getting all this ready for me!" Then, suppose he had turned to his friend and said, "My little brother is great. He is always thinking of ways to make other people happy."

Just imagine how delighted that little brother would have felt! All his preparations would have been more than worth it. This praise would motivate him to be even more loyal to his older brother, more happy to help him in any way he could, and more excited to continue his good works.

Most examples of praise in your family will not be as dramatic as this story, but your praise will be just as powerful. I cannot stress enough how important it is that you praise your brothers and sisters. A word of praise can totally change their attitude, perspective, day, and life. Praise motivates people to keep trying and not to give up. It gives hope and vision for the future. Praise shows that you are on their side and that you appreciate them. It encourages, uplifts, and motivates. Praise changes lives.

"A word fitly spoken is like apples of gold in pictures of silver." (Prov. 25:11)

"Heaviness in the heart of man maketh it stoop: but a good word maketh it glad." (Prov. 12:25)

"A man hath joy by the answer of his mouth: and a word spoken in due season, how good is it!" (Prov. 15:23)

Ways to Express Praise:

- A smile.
- An exclamation such as: "Well done!", "Wow!" or "Great job!"
- A note of encouragement.
- Explaining how God has used them to benefit your life.
- Expressing how you have noticed specific traits of godliness in their lives.

    I want to emphasize this one. Praise isn't simply a compliment. It is encouraging someone by identifying the traits of godliness they demonstrate. It is far better to praise an inward trait, such as kindness, truthfulness, or joyfulness, than their outward appearance or achievements.

- Thanking them.
- Show gratefulness for any way they have benefited you (through their actions, words, or example).
- Praising them to other people (especially to your parents and friends). Do this in the presence of your siblings so they can hear it.

Learn to focus on the good, rather than the bad, in the lives of others. When you criticize someone, they become discouraged and feel like they cannot please you. Soon they may think, "So, why even try?" It has been said that we should praise ten times for every one time we criticize. You will find that you will accomplish much more in the life of your brother or sister if you focus on praising their strengths, rather than pointing out their weaknesses. Iron sharpens iron, but a soft cloth polishes gold. Praise is that soft cloth.

A friend of mine, who is sixteen years old, was asked to baby-sit three of her brothers. As her parents left, they gave two of the boys an assignment. These boys began to complain that their other brother did not have to do any work. This young lady quickly said, "Well, your brother is always so helpful, I'm sure he'd be happy to help you if you asked him nicely." A big smile came over this brother's face when he heard her praise him. Before they even had a chance to ask him, he piped up, "I'd be happy to help!" This young lady's problem with her brothers was solved very easily because she used the amazing weapon of praise.

Instant Success

Our family lives up the street from a small park. One day, my dad walked to the park with a friend to kick around a soccer ball. A group of kids came by and asked if they could play. As they joined the game, Dad noticed one of the little boys who seemed to be the unpopular one. This child seemed to be disliked by everyone else and left out. My dad came

up with his own objective for that game—to encourage this little boy. He was on Dad's team and Dad always tried to kick the ball to him.

"Great pass!" my dad would say. This immediately gave the little boy new motivation, and he began to play harder. Dad continued to kick the ball to him and then praise him by saying, "Wow, you're really playing well!" Now the boy was really encouraged and began to outshine the other players. This gave my dad more and more opportunities to praise him. And of course, the more he was praised, the more motivated and energized he became. By the end of the game, this little boy was exhausted, but he was very excited and didn't want to quit. It had probably been the best game of his life, simply because of some praise. Everyone desires approval, so when you praise others you make them feel successful. You are elevating their name and reputation and expressing your approval of them. Have you ever realized that you have the power to make someone's day successful, simply by your praise? Also, success breeds more success. That is why a little praise will go so far.

How to Receive a Rebuke

There's another part to this chapter. Brace yourself, because this is even harder than giving praise. As we purpose to praise others, rather than criticize them, we must realize that others will not necessarily praise us. In fact, we must be prepared to receive the opposite—criticism. What do you do when your sister, or mother, or friend comes up to you and tells you that you are wrong, or that you are doing a terrible job of such and such, or that their way is better? That's hard for anybody to process. Not very many people can tolerate this or handle it correctly. But if you are able to receive rebukes in a godly way, this is a sign of true maturity and wisdom. Hopefully, you have already been working on applying humility and meekness, because then you have a head start.

"Reprove not a scorner, lest he hate thee: rebuke a wise man, and he will love thee." (Prov. 9:8)

"The eye that heareth the reproof of life abideth among the wise. He that refuseth instruction despiseth his own soul: but he that heareth reproof getteth understanding." (Prov. 15:31-32)

What Are the Two Forms of Rebuke?

1. Rebuke that is true.
2. Rebuke that is false.

We need to be able to handle a rebuke under either circumstance.

Both of these are very difficult to receive. If the one giving you the rebuke is right, then you know that you have been wrong in that certain area, and must admit your error. On the other hand, if they are wrong, then the criticism is unjust, and that's difficult, too.

One time I was driving down the road, following my dad who was driving the vehicle in front of me. We stopped to get gas and Dad mentioned to me a few mistakes I had made in my driving. My immediate response was to explain why I had done those things (defend myself). As we continued driving, I began to think about how amusing it is that everyone always, automatically, defends himself when he is criticized. I began to think of many church and family problems that happened because the person criticized was simply not able to tolerate it. Right then, I purposed that I wanted to learn the right way to receive all rebukes and criticism. I have not always succeeded in this, but I have often remembered my commitment at times when I was tempted to defend myself.

The Right Ways to Respond:

- Listen to the whole rebuke without arguing back.
- Thank them.
- If it's clear that they are right, acknowledge this on the spot. If you think they are wrong, tell them that you will think about it, and that it is important to you to be like Christ, and do the right thing.
- Carefully think it through, pray about it, and determine what God wants you to learn through the situation.
- If possible, go back to them and explain how their rebuke helped you.

Receiving A Rebuke

STEPHEN'S SECTION

A "Hot" Conference

The sun was beating down on an unair-conditioned house, where our family was having a hot conference. This was no ordinary conference, however. This was an important one. We were talking about where we were going out to eat. Actually, it was Grandma's idea to take us out for lunch. We all liked the idea, especially since she was going to pay. Grandma said, "I don't want to drive around. Let's decide first where we are going to eat." We began discussing possible restaurants. Grandma didn't want to eat at a fast food restaurant. Neither did she want to go out to some expensive, fancy restaurant. We gave her many suggestions, but she vetoed all of our ideas.

Finally, Grandma said, "Let's just drive around." We loaded everyone and their unnecessary junk into the car and took off. Grandma knew of a restaurant she wanted to try, but she didn't know the name of it. She thought she knew where it was, but when we arrived we found no restaurant. We continued driving, and telling Grandma all the restaurants we passed. She didn't like any of them. We even stopped at a few restaurants to look at the menu. None seemed to meet Grandma's requirements. We were beginning to wonder if we'd be eating lunch at all! Then we passed a restaurant called the Bohemian Garden. Since we were tired of driving around, we said, "Let's stop here." Amazingly, Grandma agreed and we went in. The restaurant turned out to be very nice; it was not too expensive, and it even met Grandma's approval.

About halfway through the meal, Dad said, "I'm sure this restaurant would enjoy some harp music. The little harp is in the car, why don't we bring it in?" We all looked at each other. Dad and his strange ideas!

Sarah said, "I don't want to play."

I stated clearly, "Don't ask me to play."

Grace (who was seven years old) said, "I'll play! Can I play? Let me play! Pleeeease! I wanna play!" Dad asked the manager and she said it would be fine. In came the little harp. Dad set it down near our table and Grace began to play. Unfortunately, there were some problems we hadn't thought of. First of all, Grace hadn't practiced for a week. (We had just come back from a weeklong conference.) She was pretty rusty. She was also a little nervous and could hardly remember the songs. Besides that, the harp had just been in a hot car and was quite out of tune. It sounded terrible. We were all embarrassed. Sarah and I pretended we were customers who had nothing to do with the restaurant's live entertainment. We were trying not to laugh.

After a few songs, Dad called Grace back to the table to finish eating. Grace said, "I'm **never** playing the harp for anyone again." Then the waitress walked over to our table. We were afraid she was going to ask us to leave. Instead, the waitress enthusiastically thanked Grace for playing, and said she was just wonderful. She told us how much the other customers were enjoying the harp music. She gave Grace a $20.00 gift certificate for our family to come back to the restaurant. Grace immediately got a big smile on her face. She hopped up and said, "I'm going to go play some more songs!"

Do you see how this one comment of praise changed Grace's whole attitude? She went from being very discouraged to being very excited because of just a little praise. Have you been using the weapon of praise? This weapon seems to be one of the best kept secrets.

But what makes praise so hard? Maybe it's because you feel that your siblings aren't worthy of your praise. Maybe it's because you're upset and you don't feel like praising them. Maybe you just don't think of praising. Whatever may be your reason, if you have not been praising, you are not using one of your most useful and effective weapons.

As you begin to use this weapon, make sure you use it correctly. We need to praise with no hidden motives. It is important to be genuine and to mean what we say. Our motive must be to give to them, without hoping to get anything in return.

Your "Top-Secret" Weapon

Picture this: Your little brother is having a bad day. He got up late and he's behind on his chores. (No, this is not about me. Do you think I would ever get up late?) Then he spilled milk on the floor and had to clean it up. He was already upset, so, when you borrowed his pencil without asking, he yelled at you. Your mom heard this and scolded him. It's just a bad day for him all the way around. He feels like nothing is going right. You have an option: you can treat him the way he's been treating you (which is only going to make his day worse), or you can try to encourage him. Now, let's just say you decide to apply this weapon of praise. (I know. I'm giving you the benefit of the doubt.) So, you begin to think of something you can praise him for. You remember that yesterday he (let's see ... what did he do? Surely, he did something nice. Well, how about the day before ...) That's it! He helped you watch your baby sister. You go to your brother and say, "I never got a chance to thank you for helping me baby-sit the other day. Did you know that because you helped me, I was able to get an important school assignment done? Thank you!"

So, when you put down this book, pick up your "top-secret" weapon and "fight the good fight!"

Stephen's Definitions

Constructive Criticism — When I criticize you.

Destructive Criticism — When you criticize me.

Family Conference — When everybody talks, nobody listens, and everyone argues about it afterwards.

Interruption — A thing which people constantly do, with one exception - when you're praising them.

Tactfulness — The ability to describe to others the way they see themselves.

Small Talk — Something that comes in large doses.

Flattery — It is like a marshmallow—there isn't much to it, but it sure makes you feel good!

GRACE'S SECTION

Amazing Weapons

Hooray! Now it's time to "Fight the Good Fight!" In order to fight you need weapons. So, get them out and let's "go for it!" This is what we've all been waiting for! Now, let's see ... Our first weapon is getting our parents on our side. Wait, no, our first weapon is learning to defend ourselves with a big vocabulary. No, that's not it ... Oh! I remember, our first weapon is learning to shoot rubber bands!

"No? ... It's not? ... All of those are wrong? ...

You say, "The weapon is *praise*"???

Well ... after reading Stephen and Sarah's sections, I guess we are all convinced that praise really is a weapon. But I want to tell you that it's not the only weapon. Since they were already so thorough in telling you about the weapon of praise, I'm going to tell you about another important weapon. It's called prayer. Have you been praying for your brothers and sisters?

The Weapon of Prayer

The most important way that we can help our brothers and sisters is by praying for them. Pray for them every day! Never think that prayer is a small or unimportant part of life. How could we ever "win" if God wasn't on our side? We'd make a pretty lousy warrior, wouldn't we? We can't do anything without the Lord. We cannot succeed in getting along with our brothers and sisters without God's help. God is the only one who can really make our family be the way He wants us to be. Therefore, if we don't ask for God's help, we aren't using our best weapon.

How Can I Use This Weapon?

- Ask your brothers and sisters for prayer requests and pray for them.
- Pray that you will have the right responses to everyday occurrences.
- Pray that your brothers and sisters will be strong for the Lord.
- Pray that they would make wise decisions and grow in their love for the Lord.
- Pray that you would develop a greater love for your brothers and sisters.
- Pray for wisdom when you don't know what to do. (James 1:5)

- Ask the Lord to show you any times you have hurt your brothers or sisters, so you can clear your conscience.
- Ask the Lord for ways you can have ministry together with your brothers and sisters.
- Ask the Lord for strength, since we are so weak by ourselves. (II Cor. 12:9)

It Happened at One O'Clock

Crash! Bang!

"Help!"

"Ouch!"

"What was that noise?" Sarah wondered, as she came racing up the stairs. She found me scared and crying hysterically, sitting in a pile of stuff. A bookshelf had fallen on me, but because I was right in front of it, I was able to catch it and push it back up. The only bad part was that all the things on the bookshelf did fall—and they fell on me! There were damaged items and pieces of broken glass on the floor, but, except for some bumps on my head and a scratch on my face, I was okay. We were thankful the bookshelf itself didn't completely fall over on me with full force! I was only eight years old and could have been seriously hurt. But don't put this book down now, that's not the end of the story.

The theme for our family that week was protection, because the night before Sarah had led a Bright Lights meeting on the subject of protection. We had been studying the topic all week. When Dad came home from Chicago later that evening, Mom asked him if he had prayed for our family's protection that day. He said, "Yes," but then he remembered that he didn't pray till one o'clock in the afternoon ...

A few minutes later, Dad noticed the Band-Aid and scratches on my head, and asked what had happened. I was just going out the door, so I said, "I'll tell you later, but it happened at one o'clock."

Wow! God prompted Dad to pray for the family's protection just when we needed it!

Prayer is powerful! Getting along with your brothers and sisters is a hard topic, and it is an impossible task to do all by ourselves! We'll never win alone! We are so helpless, but God is so strong! The Lord is on our side and He wants us to ask for His help.

"The effectual fervent prayer of a righteous man availeth much." (Jas. 5:16)

So if you are serious about making your brothers and sisters your best friends—pray!

HIS STORY APPLIED TODAY

Have You Read the Letter?

A man went to a town to preach the gospel, but the people in that town did not receive him. Instead, he was whipped and imprisoned for his teaching. When the Lord delivered him from prison, he went on to another town to continue preaching the gospel. This man had already faced much persecution and tribulation, yet he did not give up. He preached the gospel wherever he went. In this next town some people believed his message about Christ and became Christians, but others withstood his work here, too. Soon, the whole city was in an uproar. He escaped during the night and went on to the next town. This man was concerned for the new converts and wondered how they were doing. Would they stand strong in the faith? Would they endure even through persecution? Would they remember the things he taught them? He prayed for them. He also decided to write them a letter. See if you can notice how he uses the weapon of praise.

At the beginning of this letter he states, *"We give thanks to God always for you all, making mention of you in our prayers: Remembering without ceasing your work of faith and labor of love, and patience of hope."* He continues by praising them for the way they have been examples to many other believers, and explains that people everywhere are talking about their faith and testimony. In his next letter he continues, *"We are bound to thank God always for you, brethren, as it is meet, because that your faith groweth exceedingly, and the charity of everyone of you all toward each other aboundeth; So that we ourselves glory in you in the churches of God for your patience and faith in all your persecutions and tribulations that ye endure."* (I Thess. 1:1-10 and II Thess. 1:3-5)

Do you see how this was an excellent strategy to encourage and motivate these young believers? This was not flattery. Paul was not saying this for his own gain, and of course, all the praise was true. Since these were new Christians, surely there were many things Paul could have corrected in them or criticized them for. But if you read Paul's letters, you will find that he deals gently and compassionately with his disciples. He encourages them and expresses his deep love and gratefulness for them. Paul realizes that watering the little seeds of correct things will go farther than using a battering ram on the thick defensive walls of error. A battering ram **will not** knock down the walls, but praise **will** cause them to open the gates. Paul asks each one of us to follow his example. (Phil. 3:17 and 4:9)

DEAR TIM,
REMEMBER THE GOOD THINGS THE ELDERS SAID ABOUT YOU, THE PROPHECY, AND ALSO THE GIFT. YOU ARE A MAN OF GOD. GUARD THE TASK YOU HAVE BEEN GIVEN. FLEE MONEY AND PURSUE THE WAYS OF GOD. IT IS TRUE THAT JESUS SAVES SINNERS. I WAS THE WORST AND HE SAVED ME. FIGHT THE GOOD FIGHT OF FAITH.

I'M PERPLEXED...

Question: What if I can't think of ANYTHING to praise?

Answer: If you can't find anything big to praise, then praise something small. If you can't think of anything small to praise, then praise something tiny. Perhaps it is even best to praise the tiniest things, because there's nothing to praise in the action itself, and you are forced to praise the character trait behind it. This is the most important thing to praise. For example:

- **Have they smiled at you? You could praise their cheerfulness.**
  "Johnny, you smile at people a lot and that makes them comfortable. Some people never smile."
- **Have they finished their chores? You could praise their diligence.**
  "Johnny, how are you so fast at getting your chores done? Maybe you should start a chore business."
- **Have they obeyed your parents in any assignment? You could praise their obedience.**
  "Johnny, Dad gave you a hard job. You sure handled it well."
- **Have they risen early in the morning? You could praise their self-discipline.**
  "Mom, did you know Johnny was the first one up this morning? When I got up he was already at his desk."
- **Have they listened to you? You could praise their attentiveness.**
  "Johnny's pretty quick at catching on to things. Did you see how he followed all the directions exactly like I told him?"

Self-Evaluation Quiz 10

1. My main reason for not praising is...
☑ I don't think of it.
❑ I can't find anything to praise.
❑ I'm too angry.
❑ My brother and sister don't understand English.
❑ I open my mouth, but it just won't come out.
❑ I feel awkward not knowing what they might think of me.

2. I praise my siblings...
❑ At least 10 times for every one time I correct them.
❑ About 3 times for every one time I correct them.
☒ Approximately the same amount of times as I correct them.
☒ 1 time for every 10 times I criticize.

3. I praise specific character qualities that I observe in the lives of my brother/sister...
❑ Often.
❑ Never.
❑ They never praise me.
☑ I think maybe I did it once, at least I'm pretty sure I did.
❑ I have the right to remain silent.
❑ Ask me after I finish this book.

4. When my sibling enters the room I...
❑ Yawn.
❑ Cheer.
❑ Faint.
❑ Bow.
❑ Turn on the radio.
❑ Scream.
❑ Push my eject button.

5. I praise my brother/sister in front of others...
☒ Yes.
☒ No.
❑ You don't know my siblings.
❑ I couldn't think of anything to praise, even if I wanted to.
❑ Do you know where I can get my vision tested? I think I'm reading the question wrong.

6. I involve my brother/sister in projects...

☒ As much as I can.

❑ They are my projects.

❑ Only when I have to.

☒ When I need free labor.

❑ When I'm bribed.

7. When I am making cookies and my little sister wants to help, my normal response is to...

☒ Enthusiastically say, "Sure. You can do the dishes!"

❑ Say, "If you insist—but this time you better not mix in the salt instead of the sugar, drop it in the dishwater, fall asleep when they are in the oven, or feed them to your hamster."

❑ Say, "Great, I'd love to have you help!"

❑ Say, "Sure, how about you sell them for $1.00 a piece and we will split the profits?"

CHAPTER ELEVEN

Did You Say "Friends"???

Practical Ways to Build a Friendship

SARAH'S SECTION

Practical Ways to Build a Friendship

"Lord, I don't want to settle for just average in my relationship with Stephen and Grace. I desire Your best. Is there anything I could do to strengthen our relationship, get closer to them, and encourage them?"

This is what I prayed several years ago. Even though I felt like I had a good relationship with Stephen and Grace, I was wondering what I could do to make it even better. The idea that the Lord gave me at that time has been amazing to me. I am excited to share it with you. Because of the many benefits this has brought to our family, I would like to encourage you to do the same thing with your brothers and sisters.

The idea was to start a group called ATTACH. This stands for **Advancing Together Toward Accountability, Christ-likeness,** and **Harmony.** The purpose of ATTACH is to provide a "one-on-one" time for brothers and sisters to encourage each other and learn from each other. I wrote a letter to Stephen and Grace inviting them to begin ATTACH with me. Here is what I wrote to Stephen:

Dear Stephen,

You are invited to join a "group" with me. It is called ATTACH. ATTACH stands for Advancing Together Toward Accountability, Christ-likeness, and Harmony. ATTACH is for brothers and sisters who want to strengthen their relationship and encourage each other's walk with the Lord.

Please accept this invitation to a picnic with me on Wednesday. Rain date will be Saturday. It will be just the two of us.

> *Love in Christ,*
> *Sarah*

I wrote a similar letter to Grace, inviting her to a picnic a few days later. Both Stephen and Grace responded by saying they wanted to be a part of ATTACH. They came with excitement to the picnic and I surprised them with an ATTACH journal which I had made.

That was just the beginning! We have continued to have ATTACH meetings and have found them to be very special. I thought I was starting ATTACH to encourage *them*, but I was surprised how beneficial it was for me. ATTACH has given Stephen, Grace, and me many meaningful times together. It has also given us a perfect opportunity for many good conversations which we wouldn't normally have in "everyday life."

If we miss out on the friendship and fellowship of our own brothers and sisters, we are missing out on one of the biggest blessings in life!

There are many different ways to "attach" with your younger brothers and sisters but here is how ATTACH has worked in our family. Every so often (once a month is a good goal) we go out for an ATTACH meeting. We try to do something special such as go out for breakfast or go on a picnic. We eat, talk, and go through each section of our notebook. It is helpful to have a notebook, because it gives you something to do at the meeting, and it produces good topics for conversation.

The Notebook

I made three notebooks—one for each of us. The notebook can be designed any way you like. I bought medium-sized spiral notebooks, decorated them, and put tabs on them to divide them into five sections. Here are the sections I suggest:

1. **Journal:** This is for individual use at home. In it we record thoughts about ATTACH, and what we did at each meeting.
2. **Bible Study:** At each ATTACH meeting we choose a passage of Scripture to read together and talk about. In our notebook we record what we learned and the verses that stood out to us.
3. **Prayer:** We share prayer requests during ATTACH and write them down so we can pray for each other. At the next meeting we share answered prayers. Sometimes we pray together at the meeting.
4. **Accountability:** We choose one area in which we want to be held accountable (rising early, memorizing, orderliness, showing gratefulness, etc.). We write these down and purpose to check up on each other to see how it's going.
5. **Projects:** At each ATTACH meeting we choose a ministry project that the two of us plan to work on over the next few weeks. (Once in awhile we choose a big project. This book was one of them!) Other things we have done are:

   - write a family newsletter
   - invite neighbor kids over for a Bible club
   - write notes of gratefulness to others
   - design a project to encourage younger brothers and sisters
   - make cookies for neighbors

Suggestions for Leading ATTACH

As an older brother or sister, your goal for this time must be for your sibling's benefit. Pray about the ATTACH meeting before you go. Ask the Lord to bless the time and use it for His purposes. Pray that you would have a good conversation and that your younger brother or sister would enjoy it. As you talk with your brother or sister, be humble and willing to share your struggles. If you open up with them first, you will find that they will probably open up to you as well.

I encourage you to come prepared with three things to share in addition to going through the notebook.

1. Praise them by telling a specific character trait you've noticed in them and why you appreciate it.

2. Motivate them by explaining talents, abilities, or qualities they demonstrate which have great potential for the kingdom of God.
3. Minister to them by sharing an insight that you have recently learned that will be beneficial for them.

Testimony from a Young Lady Who Began ATTACH

(By Tracy, 21 years old, from Missouri)

Having ATTACH with my brother and sister has been such a blessing! I started ATTACH because I really liked the idea of setting aside a time for one-on-one fellowship with my younger siblings. I felt this would strengthen my relationship with them and encourage us to be more diligent in seeking the Lord.

It was about a year ago that I began ATTACH with my younger brother and sister. They were both really excited about doing this and looking forward to it! After my very first meeting, I could already see how God was going to use this as a tool to bring us closer. Since I have a full-time job, I don't get as much time with my brother and sister as I would like to, but ATTACH has helped me to make time for them. I have found that they are happy just because I set aside a certain time for us to be together. I like to make it even more special by taking them out to lunch or to a park. I have been getting to know them better through our meetings and we have shared fun times and profitable studies. Lately, we have been studying faith together, memorizing Hebrews 11, and reading biographies of faithful Christians from history. I am so thankful for the brother and sisters God has given me. It is truly a special relationship that He created to help us grow into His likeness. "But as touching brotherly love ye need not that I write unto you: for ye yourselves are taught of God to love one another." (I Thess. 4:9)

Whether it is through ATTACH or something else, remember that communication is essential. It is important to take the time to talk about things, share ideas, share struggles, and get advice. That's part of being best friends. Some families have problems that they have not dealt with, and therefore, they are unable to properly talk and communicate as a family. Do you know what happens when you can't communicate?

A Distant Communication Story

When I was eleven, our family went on a short-term mission trip to Hong Kong. Dad was busy with his mission work, but the rest of us took advantage of every opportunity to tour the country and try the restaurants. We got lots of practice learning directions and pushing Grace in her stroller.

When we were tired of chicken feet, squid, rice, and exotic vegetables, (we couldn't bring ourselves to eat fish eyes or snake) we would take off for McDonalds. This particular day, Mom and the three of us children entered a busy and crowded McDonalds. Ordering was a difficult task because the employees spoke Chinese (and we didn't). We sat down at our table and began to eat our meal, but we soon realized that we didn't have any ketchup for our french fries. Mom went back to the cashier to get some ketchup, but the Chinese lady did not understand what Mom wanted.

"Ketchup," Mom said.

"You want water?" she asked.

"No, ketchup," Mom repeated.

"Hamburger?" the lady guessed.

Realizing her communication was not succeeding, Mom pointed to a picture and asked for ketchup. The lady was still confused. Mom tried to illustrate with her hands the rectangular shape of a ketchup package. The lady went to get someone else to help, and finally, after several more tries, Mom got her ketchup. Mom returned triumphantly to the table and Stephen said, "But Mom, I just ate the last fry!"

Many unnecessary problems arise when you can't communicate. How would a family or marriage survive if they couldn't understand each other? What would happen to a baseball team if they got their signals crossed? Sometimes, families communicate so poorly or so rarely, one might wonder whether they even speak the same language. ATTACH is a tool that enables you to spend time together and talk in the midst of a busy schedule.

After I started ATTACH, I was so excited about it that I wanted to encourage others to start ATTACH groups. Some of the girls I teach in Bright Lights have started ATTACH with their younger siblings. They have come to me with very good reports. If you start ATTACH and would like to share a testimony about it, or if you need encouragement and would like to read about other groups, come to the ATTACH page of our website at www.brothersandsisters.net. If you would like to do something like ATTACH in your family, but simply do not have the time, then I urge you to re-evaluate your priorities!

STEPHEN'S SECTION

Keep Moving

It may seem that there are practically no ways to build a practical relationship with an impractical brother or sister. You may think this at first, but amazing things can be done if we are willing to apply some perseverance.

We are now nearing the end of the book. You have showed perseverance already by getting this far. (That is, if you didn't skip.) In this chapter Sarah and Grace have shared some practical ways to begin to improve a relationship with your family. I want to encourage you not only to start but also to keep going. Like I said in chapter one, this is a marathon and we won't win if we don't keep running. Even though we will get tired and have times when we don't think we will make it, any movement forward is important.

When we are trying to build a better relationship with our brothers and sisters, things may not always go as planned. You may read a book like this and decide to change the way you act toward your family. If you are like me, you may do really well ... for two days. But after that, things will be back to normal again. We can't expect all of our problems to be fixed overnight. Everything may be wonderful for a day or so, but when things don't improve as we had hoped, it will be easy to become discouraged. It will take time and you will be tempted to give up. You must demonstrate perseverance, determination, and courage.

How Much Farther?

Our family learned a lot about perseverance the year we took a trip to Colorado (about four years ago). You see, we had one main goal for the trip—to climb Flat Top Mountain. We had tried once before, the last time we were in Colorado, but gave up halfway. This time we were determined to make it to the top.

The day began with our morning Bible study. We chose this as our verse of the day: *"I press toward the mark for the prize of the high calling of God in Christ Jesus."* (Phil. 3:14) After our Bible study, we began to prepare for our climb. We wanted to take as little as possible so we could travel light. We decided to take our lunch and that was it! Then Dad told us that it would be very cold up on top of the mountain. He said we should take clothes for both hot and cold weather. Reluctantly, we decided to add some sweatshirts and sweat pants to our backpack. It began to look a little heavier. Next, Dad informed us that our one small lunch was **not** enough. He said we needed **lots** of food. He told us we'd be glad later. We made a few more sandwiches and threw a few more granola bars into our backpacks. Unfortunately, Dad noticed that we only had one water bottle each. He insisted that we bring a whole jug of water. We were about to leave our campsite when Dad said, "Did you bring sun screen? What about the sunglasses? Oh, and don't forget the binoculars. By the way, who has the camera and the Band-Aids?" Now our book bags were so full we could hardly zip them up. They were very heavy. Finally, at 10:00 A.M. we began our climb. We had 4.4 miles to go to get to the top of Flat Top. (Keep in mind this was 4.4 miles up.) Then, of course, there would be another 4.4 miles down.

Mile 0: As we started our climb everyone was feeling happy and strong. Grace was especially jumpy and even carrying one of the backpacks. Pretty soon Grace said, "Do you think we are halfway yet?" Just then we passed a sign that said 4.0 miles to the top. It took the next half-hour to explain 4.0 miles, in decimals and fractions, to Grace. I'm not sure she ever got it. Wow, we even do school on vacations!

Mile 1: We decided to rest at a scenic overview for a snack. Our backpacks were feeling very heavy so Dad said to take some of our extra clothes (the ones he made us bring) and hide them under a tree. We decided we'd pick them up on the way down. Hebrews 12:1, *"Let us lay aside every weight, and the sin which doth so easily beset us, and let us run with patience the race that is set before us."*

Mile 2: We decided to rest and eat lunch. We were tired. We were hungry. Dad carried one of the backpacks and the rest of us took turns carrying the other one. We had to keep focused on our goal. *"Looking unto Jesus the author and finisher of our faith."* (Heb. 12:2) We quoted Scripture as we walked, so we would forget how tired we were. We also made up a song using our verse of the day—Philippians 3:14. Suddenly, we realized that we had left the binoculars where we had eaten lunch. Oh, no! Dad said he'd go back down to get them under one condition—that we keep on walking.

Mile 3: We stopped for lunch ... again. We were sore. We were tired. We were hot. We were hungry. Dad was now carrying both backpacks. When we met strangers we shared with them our verse of the day, *"I press toward the mark for the prize of the high calling of God in Christ Jesus."* We reached the timberline. It was beautiful, but the air was thinner and that made it hard to breathe.

Mile 4: We stopped for a break approximately every ten feet. Then Grace collapsed and said she couldn't go one more step. Now Dad was carrying two book bags and one person. We kept going very slowly. Everyone was too tired to talk except to ask, "How much farther? Are we almost there?"

Mile 4.4: I was the first one to the top at 12,300 feet. We made it! We couldn't believe it. We were actually there. Everybody looked half-dead, but at least we made it.

Then guess what Dad said? "It's not very far to Hallets Peak. (An attached peak slightly to the south of Flat Top with a better view.) Now that we're here we could make it in twenty more minutes."

"Are you kidding?" puffed Mom.

"No way!" I said.

"I'll lie here till you come back," moaned Grace.

"I guess I'm out-voted," Dad conceded.

As a result of the day, we came up with three reasons for climbing mountains:

Reason #1 The lessons learned and the endurance required parallel the spiritual mountains God wants us to climb.

Reason #2 It teaches you humility. You see how big the mountain is, how small you are, and how great God is.

Reason #3 You see the view from the top. It reminds us that in life we should see things from God's perspective.

Based on the lessons of the day we concluded that, though this may be our first and last climb up Flat Top, it won't be our last mountain. God has other mountains ahead in our lives. Overcoming struggles with our siblings is one of these mountains. We need to remember that these spiritual mountains, like physical ones, also require perseverance.

Just like climbing a mountain, it is important that we stay focused on our goal—being **best friends** with our brothers and sisters. That's the top of the mountain. Just "getting along" or surviving together isn't the top. We may have to lay aside the weights (unimportant things such as our own agenda or comfort) because we are committed to a more important goal.

Do not give up! The view from the top is magnificent!

Stephen's Definitions

Successful brother — One who can get his sister to listen to logic— or anything else for that matter.

Opinion — You can have your own as long as it's the same as mine.

Bad Day — When the only thing that goes off as planned is your alarm clock.

Optimist — A brother who thinks his sister will be off the phone soon because he heard her say, "Good-bye."

Vacation — Something that begins when Dad says, "I know a short cut."

Sweater — Something that children wear when their mother feels cold.

REACHING FOR HIGHER GROUND

GRACE'S SECTION

Becoming Best Friends

As we've said before, we don't just want to get along with our brothers and sisters—we want to become best friends. How do we do that? The first item to remember is that we should be a best friend to brothers and sisters without waiting for them to be a best friend to us.

Now, think about what best friends are like. They spend time together even if they are busy. They see the good in each other and do not focus on the bad. They laugh together. Best friends are able to share their struggles, and do not have to worry that the other will speak badly about them; they trust each other. They share many memories.

My Tragic Discovery

Last summer when our family took a trip to the Grand Canyon, I was excited about taking a lot of pictures. I brought my camera and began looking for the prettiest scenes and carefully chose the best shots. I could hardly wait to get my pictures developed. On the way home, I asked a friend of mine to take a picture of me with her cat. I handed her the camera and she was about to take the picture when she said, "You don't have any film in this camera." What? No film? All those pictures were for nothing? I couldn't believe it!

I was disappointed that I lost my pictures, but I realized that a worse thing happens in many families. People take pictures because they want to remember special times, but some families never even have special times in the first place. That's like trying to take pictures without film. Some families may have photographs of their growing up years, but not have the memory of a "home sweet home." What good is a photo album without memories? How can you have memories without being together?

Want More Ideas?

Sarah already shared the idea of ATTACH, but there are hundreds of other ways for brothers and sisters to attach. I want to give you a few other examples of things that have strengthened my friendship with Stephen and Sarah.

- **Planning Surprises**

    I remember one evening, about eight years ago, when the three of

us were home alone. My parents were at a meeting so we decided to make a snack for them when they got home. We put a candle on the table and began making chocolate chip cookies and popcorn (or something like that). It was fun and a nice surprise for my parents. We all enjoyed it and began thinking of more elaborate ways to surprise my parents. Soon we were having parties for my parents nearly every time they came home.

- **Writing Notes and Letters**
  A few years ago, I wrote a note to Sarah on the computer. I had forgotten about it, but one time in a conversation she brought it up. She showed me how she had printed it out and saved it in an envelope, and told me how much it encouraged her. I had no

idea that it had meant so much to her. Most younger brothers and sisters have no idea how encouraging they can be to the older ones.

- **Laughing Together**

A few nights ago, Stephen, Sarah, and I were home alone. After our bedtime snack, we decided to try playing a piano trio. It turned out to be a disaster, but it was so funny that we all ended up on the floor laughing.

We have found that, instead of looking at each other's faults, we should enjoy them as they are. It is so much more enjoyable to laugh together about each other's differences than to be irritated by them.

- **Finding Profitable Things to Learn Together**

On my 7th birthday, Sarah gave me a little rolled up note. Inside the note I found two calligraphy pens. The note read: "This is a coupon for four, 15 minute, calligraphy lessons." I was very eager to have my first lesson. Sarah began teaching me how to hold the pen, make different strokes, and write the letters of the alphabet. It was lots of fun and a useful thing to learn.

- **Being Interested in Their Lives**

I appreciate the way Stephen pays attention to what I am doing. Whenever I am working on a project, he will come in and ask me what I am doing, what it is for, give me suggestions, and make comments. I want to encourage you older brothers and sisters to be interested in what your little brothers and sisters are doing. It is really meaningful! I should know!

HIS STORY APPLIED TODAY

This is Not Fair!

I'm sure some of you reading this book come from families that have struggled through a divorce and remarriage. You may find your relationship to be especially difficult with your stepsisters and stepbrothers.

Have you ever heard of Gilead? He had many sons, but there was one son who was looked down upon by all his brothers. He was actually a mighty man of war, but they disliked him because he was only a half brother. He had a different mother than the rest of them. When they were grown up, his brothers ganged up against him and cast him out of their family. "You are only a half brother," they said. "You shall not share in our inheritance." This son was forced to run away from home because of the cruelty of his brothers. He was a castaway, without inheritance or family. Why would God allow this? It wasn't this boy's fault that he had a different mother than the rest of his brothers!

But God had a bigger plan for this man (whose name was Jephthah). The people of Israel were attacked by the Ammonites and they needed a leader. They knew that Jephthah was a mighty warrior and they went to fetch him from the land where he was living. They requested, "Come be our captain, so we can fight against the children of Ammon!"

Jephthah said, "I thought you hated me, and expelled me from my father's house. Why is it that you come to me now when you are in distress?" Nevertheless, he returned with them and became their leader. He trusted in the Lord and the Lord delivered the Ammonites into his hand. The Lord won a great victory through Jephthah and he became the leader of all of Israel. He is listed along with the heroes of faith in Hebrews 11:32. You can read the rest of his story in Judges 11 and 12.

God loves to use the underdogs and raise them up to accomplish His purposes. He often chooses those who are humble and rejected by men. (I Cor. 1:26-29) You may feel like an outcast just like Jephthah, but remember that in each of our lives, God is the One who writes the last chapter.

I'M PERPLEXED...

Question: My brothers and sisters and I have nothing in common. What can we do together?

Answer: Often a young lady who is getting married suddenly finds herself interested in fishing or football or whatever it is that her fiancé enjoys. She is interested in his interests because she likes to be with him.

Even though we may not naturally enjoy the same things as our siblings, we should choose things to do with them that they will like. Remember that our goal is not to do what we want, but to help and be a friend to them. This is another way of showing sensitivity. It is the mature act of setting aside our own desires in order to invest in someone else.

Self-Evaluation Quiz 11

1. I ask my brother/sister for ideas and suggestions...
❑ Never.
❑ When I'm desperate.
☒ As often as possible.
❑ Are you kidding?
❑ I plead the Fifth Amendment.

2. I protect my brother/sister from wrong influences...
❑ Often.
❑ Never.
❑ In extreme cases.
☒ When I notice.
❑ What wrong influences?
❑ No, they always hang around me.

3. When my brother/sister comes home I...
❑ Stand to offer them my seat.
☒ Am happy to see them.
❑ Question loudly, "Where have you been?"
❑ Quietly excuse myself from the room.
❑ Make a face at them.
❑ Hide in my closet.

4. My excuse for not starting ATTACH is...
❑ I haven't read this chapter yet.
☒ My brother/sister was sure my suggestion was either a joke or an organized plot for spying on them.
❑ I don't need an excuse; I'm planning to start.
❑ My brother/sister misunderstood and thought ATTACH was pronounced "ATTACK."

5. When your little brother asks you to read a story to him, the best response is...

❑ Sigh and reluctantly agree.

❑ Tell him to ask someone else.

❑ Say, "Sure" and begin to read the dictionary.

☑ "Suffer the little children to come unto you and forbid them not for of such is the kingdom of God."

❑ Ask how much he'll pay you.

❑ Say, "I make appointments the first Tuesday of every month."

6. When your brother calls you a name, the best response is to...

❑ Push record on the tape player and ask, "What did you say?"

❑ Tell all your friends what he said.

❑ Find a pressurized can of whipped cream.

☑ Repay evil with good.

CHAPTER TWELVE

Are You On the Front Lines?

Having Family Ministry

Sarah's Section

Having Family Ministry

The two seas in Israel illustrate a very important truth. The Sea of Galilee has both an inflow and an outflow. It receives water and it gives water. It is a thriving and healthy sea, supporting many fish and plants. The Dead Sea, on the other hand, has an inflow but no outflow. It receives but never gives. As a result, it is dead and stagnant. No life can be found there.

Likewise, Christians who only receive, but never give, soon become stagnant. It is by giving to others and serving them that we ourselves grow. A Christian who has no ministry will be weak and feeble.

The Lord has left us on this earth because there is work to do. One who focuses on only the earthly and not the eternal will be sorry one day. He is missing the big picture. He is wasting his life and forgetting about what really counts. John 15:8 says, *"Herein is My Father glorified, that ye bear **much fruit**."* That's our goal!

Most of you reading this book are in your youth. I want to encourage you that these years have much potential for the Lord. Many Americans have the idea that teenagers always rebel. They seem to expect young people to have problems, extra struggles, and bad attitudes during those years. But that is certainly not what the Bible teaches! In I Timothy 4:12 it says, *"Let no man despise thy youth but be thou an example of the believers, in word, in conversation, in charity, in spirit, in faith, in purity."* In other words, don't give people a reason to think of you the way they think of other teens whom they don't respect.

There were many young people in Scripture who were strong for the Lord in their youth and were mightily used by God. A few of these are:

- David, who took away the reproach of Israel by killing the giant
- Daniel, who purposed with his friends that he would not defile himself
- Joseph, who properly responded to his brothers' cruelty
- Mary, the mother of Jesus, whom the Lord called "highly favored"
- John the Baptist, who prepared the way for the Lord
- We could list many more such as: Timothy, Esther, and the disciple John

We also have the example of Jesus. When Jesus was twelve years old, He went to the temple with His parents. This story is found at the end of Luke two. After the Passover, Jesus' parents were on their way home. They thought He was among their relatives and friends, but when they began to look for Him they couldn't find Him and returned to Jerusalem. It took them three days to find Jesus. He was sitting among the teachers of Israel, listening to them and asking them questions, and everyone was amazed at His understanding and answers. He explained to His parents that He needed to be about His Father's business.

Now remember, how old was he here? Twelve. Yet everyone was amazed at His understanding and answers! I know that Jesus is God, but I think this story is included in Scripture to give us an example.

Just after Christmas, when I was twelve, my dad was reading this passage. As Dad thought about this story he began to feel that, although it wasn't a command, it set a standard—a standard intended for us. He decided that it would be a good goal for every young person to be mature and trained and strong for the Lord by the age of twelve. Well, I was twelve, but I was almost thirteen because my birthday is in January. Suddenly my dad realized, "Oh, no! We only have two weeks left!" He came to me and said, "Sarah, we are going to cancel homeschool for the next two weeks and do some special projects while you are still twelve."

We concluded that it is not that a person needs to know *everything* by the time they are twelve; obviously, that would be impossible. But there are certain Biblical concepts that one can understand at twelve, and basic convictions that must be in place. A twelve-year-old really can be mature and trained and strong for the Lord, and these teenage years can be some of the best years of ministry.

The truth is that the world often will listen to youth more than to adults. Mature and wise youth stand out in today's culture; they are noticed and their voice is heard. Few youth realize this power that they have. Also, we as young people, have a lot of energy during these years and not as many obligations as adults. Therefore, we have more time to devote to the work of the Lord. Do not waste these years. They are some of the most valuable ones of your life!

Warning:

The enemy doesn't want you to be fruitful and productive during these years. His strategies to keep people from what really matters are both creative and crafty. Here are some of the things that keep people from serving the Lord:

- Focus on money or pleasure (distractions).
  God is not lacking in money. He's lacking in workers!
  (Matt. 9:37)
- Fear of failure. (I Cor. 3:6-7)
- Lack of initiative (waiting for someone else to do it).
- Lack of faith in the power of God. (Heb. 11:6)
- Lack of vision for what God wants to do through our lives.
  (Prov. 29:18)
- Focus on the earthly things instead of eternity. (II Tim. 4:10)
- Hypocrisy (sin in their lives).
- Inattention to needs around them.
- Confused arrangement of what is important. (Col. 3:1-2)

God's Primary Ministry Team

As a family, I encourage you to pray that the Lord would give you a focus on eternal things. Your family is a team that God has put together to work for the kingdom of God. At our house, we've discovered that we can do many things as a family that we would never be able to do individually. Each member of the family is important and each has different gifts. My dad is the one who comes up with the ideas (lots and lots of them!). Mom is the one who keeps us all organized. Without her help, none of Dad's ideas would be completed. Stephen helps with the behind-the-scenes details in whatever project we're currently working on. He sets up, tears down, works on the computer, runs the equipment, etc. Grace is in tune with the people around us and is sensitive and friendly. And I try to coordinate the details and keep everyone focused on the goal. Besides all this, each member of our family has different skills and talents useful for the Lord. If your family is united in prayer and vision, you will be a powerful team that the Lord will use.

I am thankful for my parents who have helped us learn to have a ministry mindset. Even when we were little, Dad began to involve us in his ministry. When we were about four years old he would take us out at holidays to hand out tracts. Then he helped us develop short presentations that we could share with others (memorizing Scripture with actions, learning a poem, memorizing a story, etc.). My mom encouraged us to have ministry in our neighborhoods by running good-news clubs or helping the elderly. One time, we hung a sheet on the outside of our house and invited neighbor kids to come sit in our yard and watch a Christian video which we projected on our wall. Learn to look at your life as ministry. God brings us opportunities to serve Him everyday. The problem is that we so often miss His opportunities. The Lord sees a much bigger picture than you do for your life. He wants to use you in exciting ways if you are willing. If you are wondering what the first step is, here are some ideas:

How to Develop a Ministry

- Develop the talents and skills God has given you and use them for Him. (Singing, musical instruments, calligraphy, computer skills, writing, sign language, baking, artwork, public speaking, counseling, wood working, hospitality, gardening, working with children, photography, medical work, mowing lawns, teaching, floral design, foreign languages, etc. Any interest or skill, however small, can be used for some witness or ministry purpose.)
- Develop personal testimonies and stories. (Your personal testimonies are one of your greatest tools.)
- Be committed to personal disciplines. (Bible study, memorization, prayer, etc.) John Wesley said, "Do not seek after a ministry, rather anticipate the fruit of a disciplined life."
- Be attentive to every opportunity God brings. (Have a ministry mindset.)
- Be a servant. (Focus on being faithful in the small things that get no recognition.)
- Take initiative. (Be courageous.)
- Learn to see needs around you. (Concentrate on doing good works.)
- Be Gospel focused. (All ministry must be Christ centered Without an eternal message there is no lasting fruit.)

Special Note: If any of you young ladies are interested in beginning a ministry working with younger girls, I have some ideas for you. Please go to the Bright Lights web page (www.brightlights.info) or contact me for more information.

Another Late Night Story

If you do the preparation necessary, such as developing talents and skills God can use, He will open up doors for you to use them. Our dad has always encouraged us to see the needs of the people around us and to take initiative to meet those needs. He reminds us to turn just everyday situations into opportunities to minister to others. Sometimes, it just takes a little creativity — like one time when our family was traveling late at night (which isn't unusual, as you already know). This time, we had just given a family presentation at a church and we needed to get back home that night.

Since we hadn't had time for supper before the presentation, we were looking for a place to eat. An hour down the road (at about 9:45 P.M.) Dad pulled off at a truck stop. He asked Mom to go inside and check it out because she is our restaurant expert. She came back and said it was too crowded and expensive. Here we go again: five indecisive, opinionated people (with only 45 minutes of quality awake time) looking for a restaurant.

There was a Denny's across the street, but neither Dad nor Grace like Denny's. (Dad and Grace are a lot alike.) Denny's seemed to be the only choice, so we decided to go there on the condition that everybody was happy. We pulled in, but already Dad was skeptical. "Why are there only a few cars here at Denny's when that expensive truck stop is packed?" This time **he** went to check it out. He didn't get very far, however, because the doors were locked. That was strange because we saw a whole group of employees inside.

A lady came to the door and said, "This is a brand new Denny's and we're having our Grand Opening at 10:00 P.M. If you can wait for ten minutes you will be our very first customers and get free dessert."

"We'll wait!" we decided unanimously. Then can you guess what Dad said to the manager? "It's a grand opening, and whoever heard of a grand opening without harp music?" Last time Dad did this he meant the little harp, so I was expecting that only Grace would play. But, no. In went two harps, since they both happened to be in the van.

You may be wondering why their grand opening was at 10:00 o'clock at night. Well, they wanted to open at the least busy time in order to work all the bugs out of their system. After all, their cooks had never cooked before. They were going to practice on us! At 10:00 o'clock the cameras flashed and there was a ribbon cutting ceremony. The harps were right by the front door and customers began to arrive. While Grace and I played, Mom, Stephen, and Dad were seated in the back of the restaurant at a clean table (which had never before been eaten on). They ordered off of new menus with no fingerprints on them. Then the regional manager came to the table to express his appreciation and to tell us to order anything we wanted from the menu because it was "on the house." My mom ordered a T-bone steak. I had a nice talk with the owner's daughter, handed out a few harp tracts, and enjoyed the meal.

There are many people God brings into our path each day who desperately need the gospel, teaching, and encouragement. Purpose to have a ministry mindset, not only in your family, but everywhere you go.

Our goal should be not just to serve the Lord *some*, but to give our *entire* lives to Him. Our goal is not just to bear fruit, it is to bear **much fruit** that our Father may be glorified. (John 15:8) We must be as soldiers who do not entangle ourselves with the affairs of normal life, as athletes who labor for the gold, and as runners who lay aside every weight that might distract them. (II Tim. 2:4, I Cor 9:24-25, and Heb. 12:1)

Life on earth is only a vapor. The "trinkets" the world offers are nothing in the light of eternity. God does not want lukewarm Christians; He desires Christians who take up their cross and live lives totally dedicated to Him. *"I beseech you therefore, brethren, by the mercies of God, that ye present your bodies a living sacrifice, holy, acceptable unto God."* (Rom. 12:1)

As you purpose to get into the battle and fight for the Lord, your brothers and sisters can be your best partners in the work. Peter and Andrew, James and John, and Moses, Aaron, and Miriam are examples of brothers and sisters serving the Lord together. God intended for siblings to be close. So much so, that He refers to Christians as brothers and sisters in Christ. Partners need to work together, to help each other, and to be united in heart and mind. We must not settle for anything less. The work is too important. There is too much at stake.

STEPHEN'S SECTION

Working Side by Side

You may be wondering, "Why are they talking about family ministry? I thought this book was about how to strengthen your relationship with your siblings." The first reason is that having ministry is one of the things that will do just that. When you work together on the same side of a struggle, it helps you become close. Instead of fighting against each other, you are fighting together with one common goal. A second reason we are writing about having family ministry is that it is the most important thing you can do together. We should do important things with best friends, and there's nothing more important than the Lord's business. And a third reason for this chapter is to help you realize how much potential your family has.

This last summer our family took a vacation to the Grand Canyon. As we were packing and repacking, Sarah came up with one of her peculiar ideas. She said that she wanted to take our chalk easel and little harp so that we could do chalk talks in the evenings at our campsites for all of our neighboring campers. Our family already has a problem of bringing too much stuff. (Or did I tell you that already?) I knew that our van would be full, but now to bring the easel and harp? I said, "No, I don't want to bring them. I thought this was going to be a vacation. I don't want to have to do chalk presentations."

Our family debated back and forth and finally, the firstborn won. (Imagine that.) Sarah's strategy was to persuade everyone else so that I would be out-voted. I did have one thing in my favor: the mini-van was already jam-packed and there was no way we could fit them in. But, the morning we left, I woke up with a surprise. Dad announced to us at 4:30 A.M. that he had fit both the harp and the easel in the van. The harp was where I was planning on sleeping. But looking back, I can see all of the doors that God opened because we brought our "tools" along. We did two chalk talks at campsites and one at a friend's house. We were also asked to do a Sunday evening service at a small church in Utah, even though we were visitors and had never been there before in our lives.

In a Christian's life there is never a vacation from ministry. You may not have the same tools as others do, but God has given you different ones. He wants you to use them. When God gives you tools and abilities, you need to have them ready to go. They won't be of any use if you don't have them with you. We have several friends who use tracts. They are able to get into many talks about Christ because they never fail to carry their tools. Having something to give a person is an effective way to open a conversation.

An ATTACH Project

At one ATTACH meeting, Sarah and I were discussing what ministry we should have.

Sarah: What if we did a chalk drawing in our driveway for some neighbor kids? (Another one of Sarah's crazy ideas!)

Stephen: That's a great idea! You do the drawing.

Sarah: What will you do?

Stephen: Me??

Sarah: How about if you do the talking?

Stephen: Me??

Sarah: You can help me with the message and invite the neighbor kids.

Stephen: Me??

I finally agreed. This is what happened the next evening:

Sarah: I don't think anyone's going to come see our chalk drawing.

Stephen: Neither do I. Maybe we shouldn't do it after all. It's kind of a lot of work to set up the easel and get out the chalk ...

Sarah: ... And get the paper ready.

Stephen: Uh-huh. I don't know if we should set it up just to draw for Grace and her stuffed animals.

Sarah: Well, I guess we should get ready just in case some neighborhood kids come. Maybe someone will come who hasn't received eternal life yet.

Stephen: Okay. We'll set it up, but I don't think anyone's going to come. I guess we'll find out at 8:30.

Well, 8:30 came and sure enough, nobody was there. So we decided we would go around and remind everyone ... just in case they had forgotten.

As we were walking back home Sarah said, "Hey, who are those people in our driveway?"

Stephen: I don't know.

Sarah: Eleven people. Wow!

Stephen: It's a good thing we set up the easel!

Sarah: That's for sure. Maybe we should do this again sometime.

Two nights later... (August 28)

Stephen: I wonder if anyone's coming tonight?
Sarah: I doubt it. No one told us they were coming ... but you never know.
Stephen: Yeah, we learned that on Thursday.
Stephen: Hey, Sarah, come look in our driveway.
Sarah: Wow! Let's get some more chairs, quick. If I knew this many people were coming I would have prepared more.
Stephen: Me, too!
Sarah: I'm glad we set up the easel!
Stephen: So am I!

In spite of our lack of preparation, the chalk talk went very well. We were able to explain the gospel to twenty-eight people. God has surprises for us sometimes.

We are learning that ministry takes initiative and we need to obey God when He gives us things to do. It's always exciting to look back and see how the Lord works in ways we didn't expect.

Stephen's Definitions

Conclusion — Something you arrive at when you are tired of thinking.

Life Goals — For most of us, the danger is not that we aim too high and miss, but that we aim too low and reach it.

Opportunity — Something that is often missed because we are broadcasting when we should be listening.

Time — The only way to save it is to spend it wisely.

Expert — Someone who can take something simple and make it sound confusing.

Temper — You can't get rid of it by losing it.

Dad's Answer — My decision is maybe—and that's final.

Kindness — The oil that takes the friction out of life.

Success — It is relative—the more success, the more relatives.

GRACE'S SECTION

Having Family Ministry

Now it is time to "fight" as a family! Once things are taken care of within the family, it is time to go out and join the battle to help other people and other families. It's easier to work as a team than by yourself, right? Our brothers and sisters can be a team with us and make ministry much easier.

I hope this chapter encourages you to make your home a ministry center and to "fight the **good** fight." If you're not sure what ministry to have, here are some ideas of things anyone can do:

- **Answer the Telephone Politely**

Rrrrring! Rrrrring!

"Good Afternoon! How may I help you?" a friend of mine answered cheerfully.

"Hello, is your Mom or Dad there?" asked the lady on the other end.

"Yes, just a minute please," this girl said and handed the phone to her dad. The lady on the other end was a saleslady, but she hardly talked about the credit card she was selling. What she wanted to know was, "Who was that sweet girl who answered the phone so nicely?" This girl's dad was able to share the gospel with the saleslady simply because of the politeness and enthusiasm of his daughter.

- **Send Homemade Christmas Cards with a Gospel Message**

- **Handle Surprise Drop-Overs Graciously**

Although it can be difficult, I think it would be good to have the goal of ministering to every person who comes into your house. Hopefully, your hospitality will not be like the following frequent occurrence at our house:

It is early in the morning. We are all still in our pajamas, doing our normal morning routines around the house, when all of a sudden we hear the dreadful ... knock, knock, knock.

Immediately, the house turns into a mad rush. — Zip — Sarah races into her bedroom and shuts the door, not wanting anyone to see her in curlers. A puff of smoke remains as I jump into the bathroom. Mom makes a dash to the other room and Dad leaps from his study location (the couch), picks up his library, and flies down the stairs. Meanwhile, Sarah is frantically pulling out the foam curlers that were in her hair, and

I am trying to figure out how I can get from the bathroom to my room without being seen, so I can change out of my pajamas. Dad is soaking his hair with water, trying to get it to lie down, and Mom is changing out of her pajamas to meet our "surprise guests." Poor Stephen (who doesn't even own pajamas and is always "presentable") is left alone in the living room to answer the door. The whole house is perfectly quiet.

Everyone hears from their escape hiding places, "Oh, hello! Come right in. No, we're not busy. This is a fine time ... No, I'm not the only one home ... the rest of my family is ... um ..."

- **Show Hospitality to Guests**
  - ❑ Greet your company with a big smile at the door and introduce yourself if you haven't met them before.
  - ❑ Help your mom with the meal by setting the table, filling your guests' water, and helping with the dishes afterward. Take initiative to clear the table and help with the clean-up. Ask your mom for other ways you can help.
  - ❑ Give the parents a chance to talk by baby-sitting or playing with the other children.
  - ❑ Have Christian items in your house for guests to look at (Bible verses on the wall, good books, etc.).

- **Have a Lending Library**
  - ❑ Collect helpful books, videos, and other materials and have them ready to share with friends, neighbors, and others who come to your home.

- **Have Ministry in Your Neighborhood**
  - ❑ Be friendly and take initiative to get to know your neighbors.
  - ❑ Rake leaves and shovel snow.
  - ❑ Give gifts—cookies, bread, cards, etc.

    One family I know was trying to think of ways to minister to their neighbors. For Thanksgiving they put some gourds in a little basket with homemade bread and a little Thanksgiving tract. They handed one out to all the neighbors on the street. They were very surprised to receive a thank you card from a lady telling how much she appreciated them. She told them how glad she was that they were her neighbors and that their family was a blessing to have on the street.
  - ❑ Be available to assist your neighbors when they need help.
  - ❑ Run good-news clubs or other kids' events.

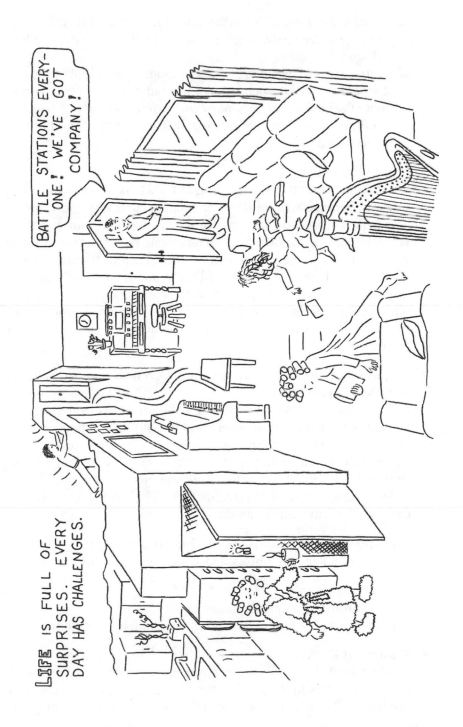

❑ Always stand alone for what is right. Make sure you are a good influence on the neighbor kids and that they are not a bad influence on you.
❑ Learn verses to use in difficult situations with neighbor kids. If other kids take the name of the Lord in vain or use bad words, quote Psalm 8:1 *"O Lord our Lord, how excellent is Thy name in all the earth!"* or other similar verses. I have found this to be very helpful.

- **Hand Out Tracts**
  Our family has found that handing out tracts is a useful ministry. It is fun because we can do it as a family and it doesn't matter how little you are. In fact, we've discovered that four and five-year-olds can be the best tract "hander-outers." We like to write our own tracts for various holidays and invite our friends to hand them out with us. St. Patrick's Day parades or Fourth of July festivities are especially good places. We found that at a parade three people can hand out 1,000 tracts in an hour. If you would like more information about tracts for holidays, you can write to our family.

- **Prepare Various Presentations for Churches, Sunday Schools or Other Events**
  This is not as impossible as you think. Use the gifts God has given your family such as musical instruments, singing, acting, or even things like cake decorating or drawing. You could learn Bible verses with actions with your brothers and sisters, act out a Bible story, find an item you own to use as an object lesson, tell a story, or learn a special musical arrangement. This takes creativity and patience, but any family can do it.

- **Minister to the Residents at Nursing Homes**
  They love music and stories and they especially love to talk to children.

- **Write Family Newsletters**
  Tell little recent stories of what God has done in your family.

- **Witness at Parks**
  I have found that parks are a good place to get to know other kids and witness to them. One time I was spending the day with my friend, Rachel, and we went to a park. As we were playing,

we noticed a girl that looked a few years younger than us. She looked kind of bored, so Rachel and I asked her if she would like to play with us. She was happy and agreed. After a little while we sat down and talked. We showed her a tract and talked to her and explained the gospel. That afternoon she prayed with us and asked the Lord to forgive her sins!

Rachel and I excitedly told Rachel's family that she got saved, and we talked about it all the way back to their house. But that's not the end of the story. The Lord had arranged for another girl who wasn't a Christian to be in the van. (Rachel's family had been babysitting her so she came along.) When she heard our story, she began to ask questions about Jesus. When we got to Rachel's house she prayed and accepted Christ as her Savior!

THE MALLY SCHOOL ROOM

Self-Evaluation Quiz 12

1. I believe it is important to be kind to my siblings...
- ☐ On the second day of every month beginning with the letter P.
- ☒ On their birthday.
- ☐ Before my birthday or Christmas.
- ☐ When we have company or the video camera is on.
- ☒ Seven days a week.
- ☒ All of the above.

2. My goal in reading this book is...
- ☐ To satisfy my parents.
- ☐ To improve things a little.
- ☒ To gain the friendship God intended me to have with my siblings.
- ☐ To finish it and give it to my brother for Christmas.

3. When you are waiting for an important phone call and your sister has been on the phone for at least an hour, the best response is...
- ☐ Stand right in front of her looking at your watch, sighing, and twiddling your thumbs.
- ☐ Write her a note saying, "This phone will self-destruct in ten seconds."
- ☒ Purpose to pass this test from the Lord even if it's hard.
- ☐ Play the trumpet in her ear.

4. If we had a family ministry...
- ☐ I'd have to do all the work.
- ☐ We'd start with a missionary project on our teddy bear.
- ☐ How can I have ministry when the doorbell is chiming, the phone is ringing, the microwave is beeping, the baby is fussing, the bread is burning, the dog is barking, and my little brother is pounding on the piano?
- ☐ The fruit for eternity would be worth it.

Little Miss Grace

Little Miss Grace
Sat in her place
Writing *Fight the Good Fight*.
She thought and she paced,
She wrote and erased,
And struggled with all of her might!

Little Miss Grace
Please don't erase!
(Or carelessly hit the "delete.")
The computer still works
In spite of its quirks
And your project is finally complete.

Little Miss Grace
Has finished the race,
Excited her joy to express.
"It's finished for real!"
She says with a squeal,
"No more of this pressure or stress."

Says Little Miss Grace,
"If your book you misplace,
Please bother Sarah—not me.
Go to Stephen to grumble,
With complaints or to mumble.
I am the youngest, you see."

Little Miss Grace
With a smile on her face,
Would like to make one last request.
I must say, "Good-bye,"
But your "best friends" are nigh,
Now it is time for your test.

TO CONTACT US:

We want to hear from you. Please send your comments, questions, and testimonies to:

Tomorrow's Forefathers, Inc.
P.O. Box 11451
Cedar Rapids, IA 52410-1451

Or email us at: info@brothersandsisters.net

For more information see our website at www.brothersandsisters.net

ACKNOWLEDGEMENTS:

Special thanks to our wonderful grandparents (David and Ann Rodgers) for being our first proofreaders and our most loyal supporters in everything we do.

We also want to express gratefulness to Kt and Elizabeth Cook, Jeff and Lu Wheeler, Uncle Larry (Rodgers), Katy Harris, Kim Wallace, Shannon Juhl, Merle Postlewaite, Dr. Dan Smith, Penny Thrasher, and the Bowman family. Thank you very much for your encouragement, proofreading, and friendship.

Thank you also to Winters Publishing for your assistance and for going out of your way to be helpful to us. We are thankful for the miraculous way God brought us together.

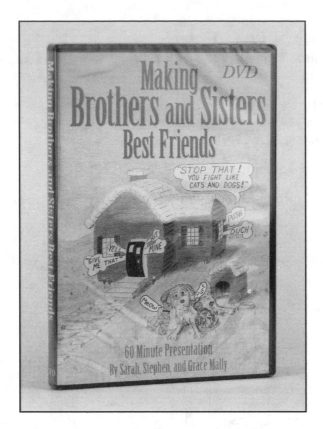

Making Brothers and Sisters Best Friends (DVD and CD)

In this one hour presentation, Sarah, Stephen, and Grace Mally share how they worked through irritations, pride, and offenses in their relationships with each other and learned to become best friends. Including funny skits, personal testimonies, insights and many of the key concepts from this book, this session will be entertaining for the entire family. It is recommended as a supplement resource to further reinforce the lessons in this book. Also useful for Sunday school classes, Bright Lights groups, or home school support groups.

By Sarah Mally

264 pages

Suggested for young ladies ages 12 to 90.

Before You Meet Prince Charming

How can young people be committed to purity and to God's best? This guide to radiant purity combines the story of a princess long ago with modern day application for young ladies today. Through this captivating fairy tale, Biblical insights, practical instruction, and lots of humor, Sarah Mally challenges young ladies to turn to the Lord for fulfillment, to guard their hearts and minds, to identify and avoid the world's thinking, and to shine brightly in this generation.

"Sarah Mally is a 'bright light' in our day—a winsome, counter-cultural young woman with a passion for Christ and for truth."

—Nancy Leigh DeMoss
AUTHOR, HOST OF REVIVE OUR HEARTS RADIO

"This book answers the big questions in a friendly, honest, and light hearted fashion."

—Dr. Jeff and Danielle Myers
AUTHOR AND SPEAKER, FOUNDER OF MYERS INSTITUTE

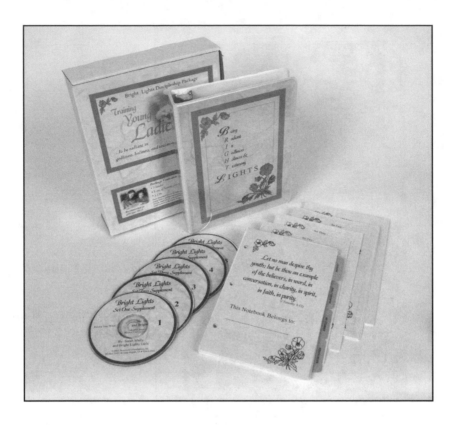

Bright Lights Discipleship Package

This discipleship course is recommended for use in a Bright Lights group, a small group setting, or for young ladies and mothers to read and discuss together. Covering many fundamental areas such as developing a close relationship with your parents, contentment, discernment, accepting the way God designed you, how to develop a ministry, controlling your words, choosing wise friends, and many other practical topics, this course is designed to encourage young ladies to use their teen years for the Lord. Each illustrated lesson contains rich biblical insights, practical applications, and testimonies from girls who share how the Lord has been working in their lives. Package includes one Bright Lights binder, Sets 1-5 (29 eight-page booklets), and 5 CDs which contain stories and testimonies.

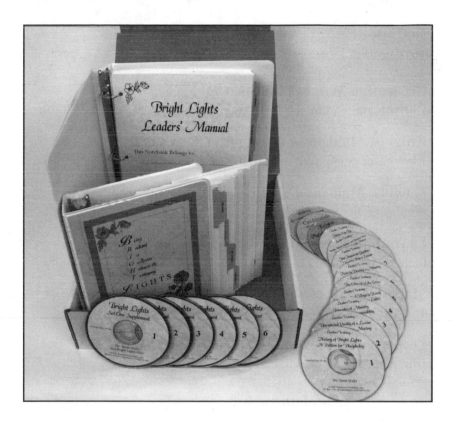

Bright Lights Leaders Training Kit

This kit was developed to provide encouragement, training, ideas, and resources for young ladies or mothers who would like to begin a discipleship group for girls in their area. It includes the full Bright Lights curriculum (see previous page) and a Leaders Manual with ideas and supplements for the teacher. The kit also includes twelve CDs of the sessions from the Leaders Training conference, covering topics such as principles of ministry, how to lead an effective Bright Lights meeting, and practical ways to reach the hearts of young ladies.

Additional Resources from Tomorrow's Forefathers

Credentials Without College CD
1 hr. presentation by Sarah and Stephen Mally

Knights, Maidens and Dragons CD or DVD
1 hr. presentation by Harold and Sarah Mally

Knights, Maidens and Dragons Supplement
Sixty page booklet by Harold Mally

Learning From Dad
Father-led series to train the family in godliness by Harold Mally

Making Brothers and Sisters Best Friends (Spanish)
Translation of the book

Preparing Young Ladies for Their Teen Years CD
1 hr. presentation by Sarah Mally

Tomorrow's Forefathers, Inc.
PO Box 11451
Cedar Rapids, Iowa 52410-1451
www.tomorrowsforefathers.com
info@tomorrowsforefathers.com

INDEX

ABOUT THE AUTHORS

Sarah, Stephen, and Grace Mally live in Marion, Iowa, where they are involved full time in their family ministry, Tomorrow's Forefathers. They speak frequently at churches and conferences, encouraging families and young people to be strong for the Lord. The Mallys often include chalk drawings and harp music in their messages.

In 2002, Sarah, Stephen, and Grace published *Making Brothers and Sisters Best Friends*. As of fall, 2006, they have sold 30,000 copies. Their book has been translated into Spanish and is currently being translated into Korean.

Sarah is the founder of Bright Lights, a discipleship ministry designed to equip young ladies to use the years of their youth fully for Christ. This ministry which began in her living room has now expanded across the nation. Over 150 Bright Lights groups have now started in 36 states and 5 countries. Bright Lights hosts Strong in the Lord conferences for mothers and daughters, trains and equips leaders of Bright Lights groups, and provides discipleship material for young ladies. Sarah also recently published the book, *Before You Meet Prince Charming*.